Human–Animal
Interactions

A SOCIAL WORK GUIDE

JANET HOY-GERLACH and SCOTT WEHMAN

NASW PRESS

National Association of Social Workers
Washington, DC

Darrell P. Wheeler, PhD, MPH, ACSW, President
Angelo McClain, PhD, LICSW, Chief Executive Officer

Cheryl Y. Bradley, *Publisher*
Stella Donovan, *Acquisitions Editor*
Julie Gutin, *Project Manager*
Stefanie Lazer, *Copyeditor*
Julie Kimmel, *Proofreader*
Lori J. Holtzinger, Zinger Indexing, *Indexer*

Cover by Diane Guy, Blue Azure Design, LLC
Interior design and composition by Rick Soldin
Printed and bound by Sheridan Books

First impression: April 2017

© 2017 by the NASW Press

Library of Congress Cataloging-in-Publication Data

Names: Hoy-Gerlach, Janet. | Wehman, Scott.
Title: Human–animal interactions : a social work guide / Janet Hoy-Gerlach
    and Scott Wehman.
Description: Washington, DC : NASW Press, 2017. | Includes bibliographical
    references and index.
Identifiers: LCCN 2016059038 (print) | LCCN 2017006480 (eBook) | ISBN
    978-0-87101-517-4 (pbk.) | ISBN 978-0-87101-518-1 (eBook)
Subjects: LCSH: Human–animal relationships—Social aspects. | Human–animal
    relationships—Psychological aspects.
Classification: LCC QL85 .H69 2017 (print) | LCC QL85 (eBook) | DDC
    591.5—dc23
LC record available at https://lccn.loc.gov/2016059038

Printed in the United States of America

This book is dedicated in
loving memory of Jazzie Hoy

Photo by Aravindhan Natarajan

CONTENTS

ABOUT THE AUTHORS

Janet Hoy-Gerlach, PhD, LISW-S, is associate professor of social work at the University of Toledo. She has extensive experience as a social work practitioner in the public mental health services system and is an avid advocate for the inclusion of human–animal interaction considerations within social work practice. Janet is on the board of the Toledo Area Humane Society (TAHS), where she developed and supervises MSW internship placements that facilitate benefits of human–animal interaction. She helped to develop the ProMedica Hope and Recovery Pet program, which places TAHS shelter animals as emotional support animals; this is one of the only such programs in the United States. Janet has provided expert witness testimony for the U.S. Department of Justice Civil Rights Department on Emotional Support Animals and has presented nationally and internationally on the therapeutic roles of animals. She lives in Toledo, Ohio, with her wife, Jen, and their son, Zane, three dogs (Henderson, Mabel, and Dawson), and two cats (Mickey Mantle and Dominique).

Scott Wehman, LICSW, has recently obtained independent licensure to practice social work and is a member of a community-based crisis response team providing emergency mental health assessments for residents of Hennepin County, Minnesota.

ACKNOWLEDGMENTS

I have wanted to write this book since I was an MSW student in 1998; to actually have written it is a dream come true. There are so many to whom I am grateful.

Many thanks to the following: My wife, Jen, and our son, Zane, for their patience, love, and unwavering support (and Jen's last-minute help with final edits!). Our dogs, Henderson, Mabel, and Dawson, and our cats, Mickey and Dominique, for their steadfast love and companionship. My parents, Tom and Joan, for their encouragement. My colleagues; my chair, Lois Ventura; and my former dean Tom Gutteridge at the University of Toledo Social Work Program, for their support of this endeavor. My students, for being inspiring in general and for their interest in human–animal interaction and social work practice. The Toledo Area Humane Society (TAHS), for welcoming the practice of social work into their agency. Gary Willoughby, for his help with historical research and readings of chapters. Susan Conda, for her vision in creating the Hope and Recovery Pet (HARP) program. Megan Brown, for being such a great partner in implementing the HARP program and MSW internships at TAHS. The Mayor's Alliance for NYC's Animals, for their innovative tool kit resource for social workers. Erika Hogan, for all of the brainstorming sessions over the years. Jerry Floersch and Jeffrey Longhofer, for mentoring me and teaching me how to write a book. Elijah Jones and Danielle Tscherne, for their help with editing the final manuscript. Scott Wehman, for being a wonderful person to write with. Our editors, Stella Donovan and Julie Gutin, for their support and patience. NASW Press, for providing us the opportunity to write this book. And Jazzie Hoy, for being my canine inspiration.

—Janet Hoy-Gerlach

1

The Relevance of Human–Animal Interaction for Social Work Practice

Human bonds with animals can be powerful, even lifesaving. While working as a social worker doing suicide risk assessments, one of this book's authors, Janet, would routinely ask each client, "What has stopped you from acting on your suicidal plans?" The purpose of this question was to evoke from each client the strengths and protective factors—specific to that person—that had helped to keep that client alive up to that point. Responses included, but were not limited to, having children, faith and spiritual beliefs opposing suicide, fear of death, not wanting to hurt loved ones, and *not wanting to leave animals behind*. Certainly, not every person Janet spoke with who was suicidal referenced having an animal who needed him or her as a reason for still being alive, but this answer was provided frequently enough that it was apparent that having an animal could be a powerful strength and protective factor against suicide for at least some at-risk individuals. Concerns about not wanting to leave an animal behind also posed some challenges in accessing inpatient mental health care for individuals who lived alone and did not have the means to provide care for the animal if they were hospitalized.

This profound connection to animals is not unique. A Google search or journal literature review will quickly yield descriptions of individuals in domestic violence situations who delay leaving for fear of their animals being harmed, individuals in disaster situations who did not want to evacuate because they were told that they had to leave their animals behind, and individuals declining to use housing shelters because they could not bring their animals. Fitzgerald (2007) interviewed a sample of survivors of domestic violence and found several participants who cited their companion animals as a major motivation to live when they

1

were feeling suicidal. Conversely, the academic literature and Internet are replete with studies, news articles, and anecdotes of the many benefits of both formal and informal connections with animals. After the horrific mass shootings of children at Sandy Hook Elementary School in Newtown, Connecticut, therapy dogs offered a source of comfort to mourners (Cunningham & Edelman, 2012, para. 2). On the basis of feedback from the Newtown community emphatically endorsing the value and necessity of the comfort derived from these dogs, Connecticut became the first state to codify animal-assisted therapy programming for trauma survivors into state law:

> Therapy dogs were an integral part of helping surviving children heal emotionally, according to Steven Hernandez, an attorney for the state legislature's Commission on Children.
>
> "They were a constant source of care, comfort and innocence," he told legislators at a committee hearing. "The dogs welcomed the children and sat with them. Their touch and sensitivity made what was almost unbearable, bearable."
>
> Proponents of the measure cited studies that have found positive health effects on children who interact with animals, such as lowered blood pressure and decreases in cortisol—a hormone associated with stress.
>
> "They love unconditionally, are nonjudgmental, are empathetic, and enjoy the company of children," said Lauren Crowley, a licensed social worker at a school-based health center in New Britain, Conn, at a committee hearing. (Wogan, 2013, paras. 4–7)

Whether through interactions with registered therapy dogs or informal daily interactions and routines with beloved companion animals, for many people, animals matter. According to the 2015–2016 American Pet Products Association (APPA) Survey—the largest demographic survey of households with companion animals in the United States—65 percent of U.S. households reported having at least one animal, and the majority of these households reported considering their animals to be family members (APPA, 2015). In our training as social workers, we are taught to understand clients within their ecologies and systems; moreover, in engaging and working with clients, we are taught to start "where the client is at." Companion animals are very often an important part of those ecologies.

In recent years, the bonds between humans and companion animals have been increasingly recognized as significant in both social work practice and educational settings (Tedeschi, Fitchett, & Molidor, 2005). Exemplars of related education innovations in social work include the University of Denver Graduate School of Social Work's animal-assisted social work certificate program (University of Denver Graduate School of Social Work, n.d.) and the University of Tennessee's Veterinary Social Work Certificate Program (http://vetsocialwork.utk.edu/). Despite such groundbreaking innovations in social work education related to human–animal interactions (HAIs), the vast majority of social work education and practice settings still do not include routine consideration of companion animals within a given human client system (Risley-Curtiss, 2010; Turner, 2005; Walker, Aimers, & Perry, 2015). Omitting the potential significance of animals in the lives of clients from social work practice misses an opportunity to effectively harness an existing strength (for example, the ability to connect with and care for a companion animal) or resource (the companionship or social support derived from a companion animal) within a given client system (Netting, Wilson, & New, 1987). Conversely, such an omission may also preclude identification of a client stressor or barrier; for instance, a client may be experiencing disenfranchised grief because of the death of a cherished companion animal (Chur-Hansen, 2010; Doka, 2002) or may be unwilling to leave an abusive relationship because she or he does not wish to leave a beloved pet behind to go to a shelter that does not permit companion animals (Walton-Moss, Manganello, Frye, & Campbell, 2005). As put by Risley-Curtiss (2013) in a call for child welfare practitioners and administrators to expand their ecological lens in practice to be inclusive of animals, it

> does not matter what they think of animals—whether they have them, like them, or not. It is the place that animals may have in the ecologies of the families (e.g., the interconnectedness of animals and humans) they serve and therefore how that may impact the 'life of the case' that is important. . . . Once this understanding is achieved, it would seem reasonable to incorporate observations and questions about the presence of animals in/at homes and the meaning those animals have for the family members into investigations and any other assessments. (pp. 121–122)

Current social work ethics, values, and guiding theoretical perspectives underscore the importance of taking into consideration the relevance of companion animals and HAI as potential strengths or stressors for a given client system, then addressing and integrating them across areas of social work practice. Within this chapter, we explicate terms such as HAI and human–animal bond (HAB); explore the current social work ethical values and theoretical perspectives that support routine inclusion of HAI within social work practice; delineate barriers and facilitators to inclusion of HAI within social work; and situate the contributions of this book within the larger moral questions, such as speciesism, facing social workers when they consider HAI.

Terminology: HAI versus HAB

Although living with companion animals may be considered by many to be a primarily modern or Western phenomenon, historical evidence indicates otherwise: Dogs and cats were kept as companions in ancient societies of Egypt, Greece, Rome, China, and Japan (Serpell, 2011). As defined within the emerging field of anthrozoology (a combination of anthropology and zoology), *HAI* entails "the full range of people's associations with animals, including wildlife, pets, therapy, agriculture, zoo, and laboratory animals" (Serpell & McCune, 2012, p. 6). The American Veterinary Medical Association (n.d.) similarly defined *HAI* as encompassing "any situation where there is interchange between human(s) and animal(s) at an individual or cultural level. These interactions are diverse and idiosyncratic, and may be fleeting or profound" (para. 1). For terminological and conceptual clarity and to maximize relevance to social work practice, within this book, we focus specifically on the following smaller subsets of HAI (see Figure 1.1): (1) HAI with animals that is considered to be therapeutic but in which there is no ongoing relationship or bond between the human and animal and (2) HAI that occurs between humans and companion animals (either naturalistically by residing together or otherwise knowing each other or through ongoing formal therapeutic interactions) who share a bond, often referred to as the HAB.

Figure 1.1: Overlap in Human–Animal Terminology

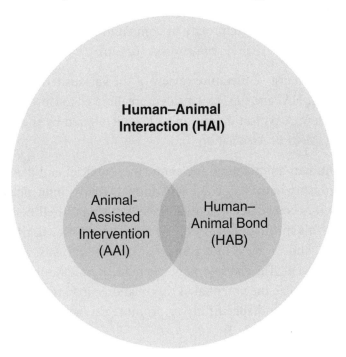

The term *bond* typically refers to close, reciprocal relationships. Although often used to refer to human relationships, it is also routinely used to describe relationships between other types of mammals, birds, and other species. The importance of mutual well-being (for both human and animal) is emphasized as a core component of the HAB by multiple researchers (Beck, 1999; Hosey & Melfi, 2014; Russow, 2002). Russow (2002) acknowledged that there is no agreed-on definition of the HAB and offered three generally established criteria to differentiate HABs from other types of HAIs: (1) There is a relationship between an individual animal and a person in which mutual recognition occurs, (2) the relationship is reciprocal and persistent, and (3) the relationship tends to promote well-being for both the human and the animal. Although such criteria for defining an HAB are relatively easy to operationalize for humans, it may be less clear with animals; as stated by Hosey and Melfi (2014),

> It would seem that there is the additional requirement to show reciprocity and an increase in well-being in both interactants. This is considerably more feasible to do with human interactants

than with animals, which presumably accounts for the paucity of studies on this. It is probably true to say that both an increase in well-being and reciprocity in companion animals is usually assumed rather than demonstrated. (p. 126)

For an exhaustive literature review of the various terms and definitions used for HAI and the HAB, readers are directed to Hosey and Melfi's (2014) review. A typical definition of *HAB* is offered by the American Veterinary Medical Association (n.d.):

The human-animal bond is a mutually beneficial and dynamic relationship between people and animals that is influenced by behaviors considered essential to the health and well-being of both. This includes, but is not limited [to,] emotional, psychological, and physical interactions of people, animals, and the environment. The veterinarian's role in the human-animal bond is to maximize the potential of this relationship between people and animals and specifically to promote the health and well-being of both. (para. 2)

Social Work Ethical Values and Theoretical Perspectives That Support Inclusion of HAI within Social Work Practice

Supporting the positive potentials of relationships between people and animals is not a role that is limited to the veterinary profession. Given that the primary mission of the social work profession is to enhance human well-being (National Association of Social Workers [NASW], 2015, Preamble section), helping to maximize the positive potentials of relationships between people and animals is a salient role for social workers as well as veterinarians. According to the NASW (2015) *Code of Ethics*, social workers are called to obtain education about, seek to understand, and promote conditions that encourage respect for social diversity; moreover, the responsibilities of social workers to promote client well-being and to respect and support clients' right to self-determination are explicitly stated (NASW, 2015, Preamble section). Features of social diversity include, but are not restricted to, race, ethnicity, national origin, color, sex, sexual orientation, gender identity or expression, age, marital status, political belief, religion, immigration status, and mental or physical disability (NASW, 2015, Ethical Standards section). Social diversity can be more broadly understood as "all of the ways that people within a single culture are set apart from each other" ("Social Diversity," n.d., para. 1). Generally understood definitions of social diversity are inclusive of ethnicity, lifestyle, religion, language, tastes, and preferences ("Social Diversity," n.d.). HAI and the HAB, along with the meanings humans ascribe to such interactions and bonds, can be significant positive or negative aspects of clients' lifestyles and social experiences.

Human clients may identify animals as family members (Turner, 2005), consider animals to be vital parts of their support networks (Wood et al., 2015), and grieve on the death of an animal (Rujoiu & Rujoiu, 2013; Turner, 2003). Children have included animals within family drawings (Kidd & Kidd, 1995) and identified animals as important confidantes in their social networks (McNicholas & Collis, 2001). At a neighborhood level, the presence of companion animals in households has been found to increase the number of positive interactions between neighbors (Wood et al., 2015) and has been identified as social capital (Arkow, 2015a). HAIs have a social component; HAIs can and should be understood and responded to within the context of a client's unique social diversity.

Several theoretical models used in social work further support the inclusion of HAI in practice: ecosystems theory, family systems theory, and the strengths perspective (Risley-Curtiss, Rogge, & Kawam, 2013). As explained by Zastrow and Kirst-Ashman (2007), two widely recognized authors of social work education texts, a system is defined as "a set of elements that are orderly and interrelated to make a functional whole. A large nation, a public social services department, and a newly married couple are all examples of systems" (p. 12). System theories are described as "concepts that emphasize interactions and relationships among various systems, including individuals, families, groups, organizations, or communities" (Zastrow & Kirst-Ashman, 2007, p. 12). As cited in Zastrow and Kirst-Ashman (2007), Beckett and Johnson defined ecosystems theory as "systems theory used to describe and analyze people and other living systems and their transactions" (p. 14). Given that nonhuman animals are living beings that interact with human systems in ways that may affect the

human systems, such transactions clearly fall within the purview of ecological systems theory application in social work practice. These animals
may also be explicitly identified by a client to be part of his or her family
system. Family systems theory, an extension of systems theory applied to
family units, is widely used to understand families in social work practice.
Given that the majority of households with companion animals identify
the animals as family members (APPA, 2015), social workers are very
likely to encounter clients who identify companion animals as part of
their family systems. Simply put, a human–animal relationship may be
a key aspect of a client's ecology or self-defined family system. Incorporating such relationships into social work assessment and intervention
enables social workers to address them as appropriate, for example, as
strengths, stressors, or both for a given client.

HAI and the HAB can benefit humans in many ways. For example, in
the beginning of this chapter, we briefly described how Janet encountered
clients who refrained from acting on suicidal ideations because they did
not want to leave their companion animals behind. In these instances,
HABs were powerful client strengths that could be drawn on to help
evoke motivation to live. The strengths perspective as used in social work
practice "focuses on client resources, capacities, knowledge, abilities,
motivations, experience, intelligence, and other positive qualities that can
be put to use to solve problems and pursue positive changes" (Zastrow
& Kirst-Ashman, 2007, p. 6). Chapter 3 of this book extensively details
the physical, psychological, and social benefits of HAI and frames these
as potential client strengths to be proactively identified and built on in
social work assessment and intervention. The presence and meaning of
animals in a client's life are not routinely explicitly asked about in suicide
assessment, yet anecdotal evidence suggests companion animals may be
a powerful and underidentified protective factor in suicide intervention.
It is imperative that potential client strengths—especially when such
strengths may be extremely salient for a given client—not be overlooked
in social work practice. Routine consideration of HAI and the HAB in
social work assessment and intervention ensures that such potential client strengths will not be overlooked, underused, or outright ignored.

Barriers to and Facilitators of Inclusion of HAI within Social Work

Given such compelling rationales for routine inclusion of HAI consid-erations within social work practice, it may seem odd that the majority of social workers are not addressing HAI (Risley-Curtiss, 2010). Risley-Curtiss, in a 2010 national study, found that one-third of social workers included questions about companion animals and other animals in intake assessments, and less than a fourth of social workers addressed HAI con-cerns in their interventions. She also found that the majority of these social workers had no training or coursework enabling them to include HAI within their practice. Through additional analysis, Risley-Curtiss et al. (2013) considered how particular factors affected four distinct ways HAIs were incorporated into practice: inclusion of questions about ani-mals in intake assessments, inclusion of animals in interventions (also known as animal-assisted intervention [AAI]), treatment for animal abuse, and treatment of animal loss. As shown in Table 1.1 on page 10, the single factor associated with increased inclusion of HAI across all four practice areas is knowing other social workers who include HAI considerations in their practice.

Hence, each individual social worker has the capacity to influence other social workers to address HAI considerations and can ultimately help to transform the profession into one that routinely considers and addresses such potentially integral aspects of clients' ecologies.

Barriers to inclusion of HAI in social work include but are not limited to lack of knowledge, staff, time, and administration-initiated direction; preformatted fields on forms available through current electronic soft-ware; issues of confidentiality; and speciesism (Risley-Curtiss, 2010). A lack of knowledge can be rectified by infusing HAI in social work cur-riculum, supervision, and continuing education and informally sharing HAI-related resources among social workers. Staff and time shortages are ongoing plagues in most areas of social work practice; social workers are often expected to do too much with too little, and having to attend to the additional component of HAI could be perceived as burdening already overworked social work practitioners. Using existing resources to smoothly and usefully integrate HAI considerations into existing practice

Table 1.1: Factors Associated with Addressing Human–Animal Interaction (HAI) in Social Work Practice

Practitioner Factor	Type of HAI Practice Inclusion			
	Assessment Questions	Animal-Assisted Intervention	Treatment of Animal Abuse	Treatment of Animal Loss
Serves primarily the children	✓			
Serves primarily elderly	✓			
Serves primarily nonelderly adults				✓
Has information on human–animal violence interconnections	✓	✓		
Has information on HAI benefits to humans		✓		
Has information on treating animal loss issues		✓		✓
Has information on treating animal abuse	✓		✓	
Asks about HAI in assessment				✓
Experience treating clients for animal loss	✓		✓	
Experience treating clients for animal abuse				
Experience including animals in interventions			✓	✓
Has specialized training in including HAI in practice		✓		
Knows social workers who include HAI issues in practice	✓	✓	✓	✓
Has own companion animal(s)		✓		✓
Wants to know more about HAI issues in practice	✓	✓		

Source: Adapted from "Factors Affecting Social Workers' Inclusion of Animals in Practice," by C. Risley-Curtiss, M. E. Rogge, and E. Kawam, 2013, *Social Work, 58*, pp. 156–160.

contexts can help to smooth such transitions (Risley-Curtiss, 2010). Administrative support and direction is also crucial in addressing time and staff shortages. Dissemination of information on the benefits of HAI inclusion in practice needs to continue to occur to engage agency leaders in adopting and supporting such practices. Electronic forms with prefor-matted fields may pose challenges in including HAI content; engaging with IT staff and considering practices such as use of supplemental fields or scanned documents may help mitigate this problem. Confidentiality may pose a challenge when a client is engaging in animal abuse or neglect; chapter 4 in this book explores in depth how the NASW *Code of Ethics* and existing reporting laws can provide guidance in such matters.

The implementation of any new practice or practice change typically involves one or more of the challenges described above; however, social work practice is necessarily dynamic rather than static. It is incumbent on social workers to continually improve social work practice by incorporat-ing new knowledge and skills—including knowledge and skills related to HAI—so that the mission of the profession, to enhance human well-being, will ultimately be better fulfilled. The inclusion of HAI consideration in social work practice also enables social workers to improve the well-being of nonhuman animals; although nonhuman animals are not explicitly mentioned in the NASW (2015) *Code of Ethics*, the code does contain numerous references to social workers' responsibilities to the broader society. Given the interconnections between violence toward animals and violence toward humans—addressed in detail in chapter 5 of this book—the Federal Bureau of Investigation (FBI) recently began treating animal abuse offenses as crimes against society and counting such offenses alongside felony crimes such as arson, assault, and homicide (FBI, 2016); it is not a stretch for the social work profession to do the same.

Larger Ethical Questions: Speciesism and Social Work Consideration of HAI

As elucidated throughout this chapter, compelling rationales exist for the routine inclusion of HAI within current social work ethics codes, values, and theoretical perspectives. However, these rationales are embedded primarily in the assumption that consideration of HAI is necessary in social work practice because of concern for human well-being. The responsibility of the social work profession toward the well-being of nonhuman animals, in and of itself, is a larger question emerging in various venues. Specifically, the question of how social work should respond to speciesism has been posed. Hanrahan (2011), writing from a critical antioppressive social work practice paradigm, explicitly called for social work to expand its value framework so as to include efforts toward eradicating speciesism and its counterpart of anthropocentrism (automatically prioritizing human animals over other animals). Through such an expansion of values, Hanrahan (2011) argued, the potential of the social work profession to enhance well-being for humans, animals, and the planet would be increased.

As explicated by Ryan (2014), the word *speciesist* was "coined in 1970 by clinical psychologist Richard Ryder (1983) and popularized by Singer to describe those who treat sentient and morally equivalent beings differently on the basis of species alone, rather than giving them equal consideration" (p. 68). Speciesism is essentially discrimination based on species. Peter Singer, author of the 1975 book *Animal Liberation: A New Ethic for Our Treatment of Animals*, which widely influenced the trajectory of the animal liberation movement, acknowledged that there were differences between humans and other animals that should give rise to some differences in the rights that each have. In particular, Singer argued that capacity to suffer (for example, to experience distress or pain) should be the benchmark for moral consideration of interests (P. Singer, 1975). As put by philosopher Jeremy Bentham (1789), "The question is not, Can they reason? Nor Can they talk? But, Can they suffer?" (pp. 235–236).

Ryan, in his 2014 seminal edited book titled *Animals in Social Work: Why and How They Matter*, offered an outstanding examination of the moral and ethical arguments for consideration of the well-being of other species within and across areas of social work practice. Ryan (2014), along with numerous other social work scholars, argued that the profession of social work emerged through efforts to protect and assist those who were vulnerable and institutionally marginalized by existing laws and policies; therefore, the social work ethical principle of respect must be extended to encompass nonhuman as well as human animals. Specifically, Ryan explicated the importance of valuing and protecting vulnerable beings, including nonhuman animals, as a moral imperative within social work practice, and he grounded this imperative in a series of chapters authored by social workers in different areas of social work practice. Distinguishing between humans and animals is a false dichotomy, as humans are mammals; for ease of terminology and reading, we hereafter refer to nonhuman animals as *animals* while acknowledging the flaws and biases inherent in this language choice. In keeping with the progressive view on animals as sentient beings rather than inanimate property, we avoid using the term "ownership" and its derivatives unless doing so is contextually necessary. For us to revisit the arguments Ryan has rigorously and passionately presented is both redundant and beyond the scope and focus of this book. We concur with Ryan's transformative conclusions and urge readers to review and consider his work.

The purpose of our book is to equip social workers to understand the importance of and routinely include HAI considerations across social work practice settings, with the hope of improving the well-being of both humans and animals. Given existing empirical and theoretical knowledge and the current NASW (2015) *Code of Ethics* guidelines pertaining to social workers' responsibilities to their clients and broader society, the social work profession is currently ethically obligated to consider HAI in practice. Irrespective of whether a social worker cares about animals and whether or not that social worker thinks speciesism should be included in social work ethics codes, one indisputable fact demands routine consideration of HAI in social work practice: For many human clients, animals matter.

2

Human–Animal Interaction within the Social Work Profession: A Historical Overview

Although the need to include HAI considerations within routine social work practice is gaining increasing attention in the profession, the call to do so is not a new one. The first known peer-reviewed article recognizing that animals are relevant within clients' social environment depicted a case study authored by medical social worker Gerda Bikales and published in *Social Work* in 1975. Bikales titled her 1975 case study "The Dog as 'Significant Other'" and described her client and the client's dog as follows:

> Lacey is a mutt. Like her mistress [Mrs. F.], she is gray, dumpy, elderly, slow, non-descript. Although there is nothing remarkable about this dog, she does have a particular distinction. She is an active case work client in a reputable community agency. (p. 150)

Bikales outlined her struggles as a social worker to assist Mrs. F. and Lacey; on consulting with colleagues about whether they had had experiences trying to assist clients with their animals, Bikales stated she had found a "sleeper in casework practice . . . a quick check with colleagues and other nursing homes confirmed that these were not isolated instances but an integral part of many caseloads" (1975, p. 150).

Indicating that the case of Lacey and Mrs. F. illustrated the conundrum, Bikales (1975) introduced their scenario as follows:

> Mrs. F. was brought to the emergency room of a local hospital . . .
> it was learned that Mrs. F., who was a widow of 82, lived alone in
> a nearby apartment building which houses many senior citizens

and whose sole companion was her dog, Lacey, about whom she made repeated inquiries. Her only financial support was a meager pension. . . . Mrs. F. had apparently fallen and lain helpless on the floor for a long time until Lacey's whines and barks attracted a neighbor's attention. . . . An examination showed her to be severely undernourished and suffering from the long-term effects of neglect. . . . She was in a chronic state of senility—incoherent, incontinent, and unable to care for herself. . . . Throughout her stay in the hospital, Mrs. F. was coherent only intermittently, but she remained constantly in touch with reality on the subject of Lacey. . . . Her mounting anxiety about the fate of poor Lacey, left to starve in an empty apartment, motivated the social worker to make the dog a prime focus of intervention. (p. 150)

Through outreach to Mrs. F.'s superintendent, Bikales discovered Lacey was no longer at the apartment. Bikales was then able to locate Mrs. F.'s niece, who reported an "embittered relationship" with Mrs. F. but indicated she had felt pity for Lacey and taken her home briefly before surrendering her to the local humane society, where Lacey would be destroyed unless someone could pay a $3.00 per day fee. Bikales was able to update Mrs. F. on Lacey's whereabouts, but she could not guarantee Lacey's continued well-being:

The social worker was able to reassure the patient that her dog was well at the moment, carefully avoiding any reference to the future. Mrs. F. cried with relief and spoke movingly about Lacey—"my only friend", "we look after each other", "it's just us old ladies, together". . . . Because Mrs. F. worried constantly about her dog and was skeptical of any reassurances, the social worker visited the shelter and had herself photographed with Lacey. This slightly blurred picture became the prime focus of the patient's hopes for her future and occupied the place of honor on her night table. (Bikales, 1975, p. 151)

Bikales was able to access Mrs. F.'s pension fund initially to cover Lacey's fees, but when Mrs. F. improved to where she could be discharged to a nursing home, she was eligible for Medicaid and her pension funds were confiscated by the welfare board. No funds were available to cover Lacey's daily care fees, and Lacey was euthanized. Mrs. F. died shortly thereafter.

One has to wonder to what extent the fates of Lacey and Mrs. F. were intertwined. Although not explicitly stated, it can be surmised that Mrs. F. perhaps gave up hope; Bikales (1975) did explicitly state that Lacey was the "prime focus of the patient's hopes for her future" (p. 151). Through her work with Mrs. F. and Lacey, Bikales (1975) stated that she gained "valuable insight and a determination to work out strategies to convince people of the importance of pets to many clients" (p. 151). Although earlier social work literature does include brief mentions of animals, Bikales was the first to explicitly call for the inclusion of HAI within routine social work practice. In this chapter, we trace the emergence of HAI considerations within the social work literature and profession. Certainly social workers are informed by a vast body of interprofessional literature related to HAI; however, by viewing HAI through a social work–focused historical lens, social workers can better understand the emergence and importance of HAI inclusion within the social work profession.

The 1960s: Violence toward Animals as Pathology and the Therapeutic Benefits of HAI

Before the Bikales (1975) case study, HAI manifested in the social work literature primarily in two ways: the identification of violence toward animals as an example of an unmet social and psychiatric treatment need (Errera & Richmond, 1961) and the identification of the therapeutic nature of HAI (Mehta, 1969). In an article depicting the lack of treatment available for children in foster care, Errera and Richmond (1961) described violence toward animals as an example of an unaddressed social and psychiatric issue among the high caseloads of foster children:

> Within this number may be found every imaginable sort of social and psychiatric problem. For example, some time ago a pet peacock was strangled by a 9 year old child. The community became aroused: how could anyone want to destroy such a delicate creature? Money was promptly raised to buy another pet,

and the new peacock was introduced to the nature center with much pomp and newspaper coverage. What about the 9 year old "criminal"? His mother had repeatedly shown she could not care for him; his father was nowhere to be found. . . . He was committed, therefore, and became another state ward. . . . All the activity has been in trying to place him somewhere. Nobody with the necessary skill and time has tried to help him with the inner conflicts that dramatically manifested themselves in this destructive outburst. (pp. 96–97)

Numerous social workers since Errera and Richmond (1961) have identified abusive behavior toward animals as a potential psychiatric symptom, and assessment of such behavior is routine in current mental health practice. Cruelty toward animals is currently listed as a symptom of conduct disorder and antisocial personality disorder, according to the *Diagnostic and Statistical Manual of Mental Disorders* (5th ed.; DSM-5; American Psychiatric Association, 2013); the DSM-5 is widely used by social workers and other mental health professionals in diagnostic assessment work in the United States. In chapter 6 of this book, we explicitly consider the link between violence toward animals and violence toward people.

Consideration of the therapeutic benefits of HAI first manifested in social work literature in the *Indian Journal of Social Work* in 1969. Mehta (1969) authored a case study of a three-year-old with separation anxiety being treated at a child guidance clinic in Bombay. Mehta described efforts as follows:

The therapist was faced with trying to treat a 3¼-yr-old child whose high level of separation anxiety interfered with individual treatment. By having the child observe domestic animals in a neighboring yard, instead of forcing her to come directly to the clinic play-therapy room, the anxiety was overcome and treatment facilitated. Therapists are advised to "be mentally alert and explorative to find out new tools of treatment." (p. 400)

The first recorded place in which animals were thought to interact therapeutically with humans far predates Mehta's 1969 case study. The York Retreat in England was founded by Quakers in 1792, and patients residing there cared for the animals as part of their treatment (Netting et al., 1987). Spiritual healing and benefits of HAIs among indigenous cultures can be traced back to ancient times (Serpell, 2010). Within the social work profession, Mehta explicitly identified interaction with animals as a way to enhance therapeutic engagement; this is now a widely recognized strategy within AAI literature. Currently, a vast interprofessional literature describes links between HAI and human well-being; chapter 3 in this book details benefits of HAI as related to social work practice. AAI has been increasingly embraced in social work practice and education; chapter 9 in this book addresses therapeutic roles of animals within social work.

Although not explicitly related to HAI, Miller and Ashmore's 1967 call for social workers to use concepts from ethology—the scientific study of the social life of animals—to better understand human functioning is noteworthy in that it underscores the similarity in social functioning between human and nonhuman animals. Miller and Ashmore (1967) suggested that analytic units used in ethology could be useful in understanding human clients: "Analytical units describing social behavior, hierarchical order, territoriality, the daily pathway, child-rearing techniques, sexual habits, and feeding behavior are suggested for application to certain aspects of the social worker-client relationship" (p. 60).

The 1970s and 1980s: The Emergence of Veterinary Social Work, the Value of HAI for Older Adults, Grief and Animal Loss, and Human–Animal Support Services

In the two decades following the case study authored by Bikales (1975), numerous additional elements of HAI emerged as areas of consideration for practice within social work literature. Specifically, the following areas of practice concern were noted and explored: the need for social workers to assist human clients in veterinary practices, the value of HAI in home settings for older adults, the need for human–animal support services (as initially called for by Bikales, 1975), and the need to support people after the death of a companion animal. In 1980, Ryder and Romasco presented a paper at the Symposium on the Human-Companion Animal Bond in

London; their paper focused on establishing a social work service in a veterinary hospital and was subsequently published in a 1981 edited volume by Bruce Fogle titled *Interrelations between People and Pets* (Ryder & Romasco, 1981). Quackenbush (1981) published a short article in an educational journal on veterinary small animal practice titled "Pets, Owners, Problems, and the Veterinarian: Applied Social Work in a Veterinary Teaching Hospital"; in this article, Quackenbush indicated that veterinary social work services were implemented in the Veterinary Hospital of the University of Pennsylvania in 1978. In a veterinary journal, Ryder (1985) iterated the benefits of animals for elderly clients and called for the evaluation of a "people-pet program" to better inform planning for such services. Collaboration between veterinarians and mental health care providers, including social workers, was also suggested as a way to improve mental health care access for people with companion animals (Crocken, 1981).

Collaborations between social workers and veterinary professionals have continued to expand widely since these chapters and articles were published, and veterinary social work is increasingly being recognized as a distinct area of practice. Elizabeth Strand founded the Veterinary Social Work Certificate Conference for graduate social work students in 2002 at the University of Tennessee in Knoxville (Clayton, 2013). Many veterinary teaching hospitals in the United States now employ social workers to assist both veterinarians and human clients. Chapter 10 in this book describes social work practice within veterinary settings.

Knoxville was also where social worker F. Ellen Netting and an interprofessional team of colleagues pioneered a companion animal placement program for older adults. The purposes of the placement program were twofold: first, to assist the home health staff in engaging with elderly clients in their homes; second, "it was hoped that the clients who requested pets would benefit from having a companion animal" (Netting, Wilson, & New, 1984, p. 182). Netting et al. (1984) described the rationale for this placement program as follows:

> The Knoxville Tennessee program was designed to place pets with community-bound elderly receiving in-home services. . . . In-home service recipients were considered to be at high risk of institutionalization, and the intervention of a companion animal

might prove helpful to some persons who liked animals. At the initiation of the project, the staff was unaware of any program in the United States that was carefully evaluating the placement of pets with urban, community-based, elderly, in-home service clientele. (p. 182)

Netting et al. explicitly listed among the goals of this program the intention to improve the quality of life of both the elderly human clients and the animals involved in the study (1984, p. 183). In their findings, they reported that depending on the severity of disabilities and illnesses of the clients receiving in-home services, pet placements could be stressors as well as supports (Netting et al., 1984). Among clientele in their home health client population who already had companion animals,

> many expressed fears of being hospitalized and concern for the pet's fate should something happen to them. For these persons it seems important for in-home service providers to be aware of these fears and to develop services such as temporary foster care while clients are hospitalized. Support services for companion animals that belong to clients might be a priority over providing new pets. Of those persons who owned pets, they described their level of attachment as high, and indicated that they would not give up their companions even if someone promised to take good care of them. (p. 189)

These 1984 findings from Netting et al. underscore those in the Bikales (1975) case study about Lacey and Mrs. F.; for older adults who have companion animals, addressing animal-related concerns must be explicitly considered a potential area of need within social work assessment and intervention. In 1984, Quackenbush and Glickman published an article in *Health & Social Work* that outlined practice considerations for supporting people in adjusting to the death of a companion animal; they similarly concluded that grief from the loss of animals is routinely underaddressed in social work practice. Chapter 8 in this book explores specific types of companion animal loss, including loss as a result of moving into a facility, as well as emerging human–animal support services that can prevent or ameliorate the detrimental impact of such losses.

In 1987, Netting et al. published a compelling article in *Social Work* titled "The Human-Animal Bond: Implications for Practice" in which they delineated social work theory, exchange theory, and lifespan development theory as relevant and applicable to HAI encountered within social work practice. Netting et al. (1987) identified seven specific ways in which social workers can "contribute to the human-animal bonding movement" (p. 63), paraphrased as follows:

1. Social workers can collaborate with animal professionals to ensure optimal results related to animal handling issues are addressed in the development of animal-related programming.
2. Social workers can acknowledge both the potential problems and the potential benefits associated with animal-related programs.
3. Social workers can assess human clients to determine their responses, including potential benefits and stressors, related to interventions involving animals.
4. Social workers can link veterinary medicine practitioners into the human services referral network so that appropriate referrals can be made.
5. Social workers can be "sensitive in counseling clients who have pet-related problems. The literature on human-animal bonding is sensitizing numerous professionals to the importance that pets play in many clients' lives" (p. 63).
6. Social workers can be aware of client–animal relationships and can assist in locating support services that include animal care.
7. Social workers can be aware of policies that affect living with animals, such as lease restrictions, so that they can advocate for clients' self-determination in having companion animals.

Netting et al. (1987) concluded by identifying social work as a profession in which social workers continually seek "ways to improve the quality of life of persons who have overwhelming obstacles. To those clients who could benefit from an animal companion, a social worker may be able to facilitate a new, or support a long-established, relationship" (pp. 63–64). The need for a broad focus on supporting clients who have animals, initially called for by Bikales in 1975, was reiterated and expanded by Netting et al.

The 1990s: Continued Exploration of HAI and Human Well-Being, and Connecting Violence toward Animals and Violence toward People

In the 1990s, social workers further explored aspects of how HAI is related to human well-being and revisited and addressed connections between violence toward animals and violence toward people. Watkins (1990) and Costin (1991) clarified connections between human welfare and animal welfare history by revisiting the historical account of Mary Ellen, the child who, in 1874, became the first documented youth to be removed from her family's home as a result of child abuse charges. These charges were facilitated through the efforts of Henry Bergh, the director of the New York–based American Society for the Prevention of Cruelty to Animals (ASPCA). In their groundbreaking book *Cruelty to Animals and Interpersonal Violence: Readings in Research and Application*, Lockwood and Ascione (1998) offered an in-depth, interprofessional analysis—inclusive of social work content—about cruelty toward animals as a component of interpersonal violence. J. S. Hutton (1998) specifically addressed diagnostic consideration of animal abuse within social work practice. In chapter 6 of this book, we delineate and address aspects of the connection between violence toward animals and violence toward humans in terms of relevance for social work practice.

Sable (1995) integratively conceptualized social workers' understanding of how humans could benefit from the human–animal bond using Bowlby's (1969) attachment theory and the six aspects of social support provided through relationships—collectively referred to as the *provisions of social relationships* (Weiss, 1974)—within a life cycle perspective. The provisions of social relationships identified by Weiss (1974) and related to social support were attachment, social integration, reassurance of worth, alliance, guidance, and opportunity for nurturance. Sable (1995) considered these elements in terms of how they could potentially be derived from companion animals. Mallon (1994) inductively found similar social dimensions of HAI benefits through a mixed-method exploratory study of the experiences of children who interacted with farm animals at a residential treatment center. In this study, published in *Child and Adolescent Social Work Journal,* Mallon (1994) reported the following:

> Respondents indicated that they spoke to the animals without fear that what they said would be repeated; that they visited the animals to feel better when they felt angry or sad; and that they learned about nurturing and caring for other living things. (p. 455)

In chapter 5 of this book, we explicitly consider the ways in which animals become part of human social systems and provide support across the human life cycle.

Innovations were also under way in social work education, with regard to the development of courses pertaining to HAI benefits and social work practice. As indicated by the University of Denver's Institute for Human-Animal Connection (2016), in 1996,

> in response to suggestions by students and alumni interested in exploring human-animal interactions, Clinical Professor Philip Tedeschi taught the first course in animal-assisted social work to Master of Social Work (MSW) students at the University of Denver Graduate School of Social Work. (Timeline, para. 1)

This has since culminated in the University of Denver Graduate School of Social Work being one of the only programs in the world to offer an HAI specialization (first offered in 2002) alongside an MSW degree (Institute for Human-Animal Connection, 2016).

The 2000s and Beyond

Aspects of HAI described in previous sections continue to be developed and expanded within social work, and additional aspects of HAI relevant for the social work profession continue to emerge. Such aspects include but are not limited to

- calls for social work consideration of speciesism as a social justice issue (Hanrahan, 2011; Ryan, 2011, 2014; Wolf, 2000)
- the need to consider how human diversity relates to HAI (Risley-Curtiss, Holley, & Wolf, 2006)

- the importance of addressing HAI concerns in domestic violence situations (Faver & Cavazos, 2007; Faver & Strand, 2003a, 2003b)
- the value of incorporating AAIs on a more widespread basis within social work education (Tedeschi et al., 2005)
- the need to add explicit questions about HAI to social work assessments (Reed, 2000)
- the need to assist clients with the inclusion of companion animals in advance directive planning (Digges, 2009)
- the need to respond to individuals who are homeless and have animals (Cronley, Strand, Patterson, & Gwaltney, 2009)
- research studies on social work inclusion of HAI within practice (Risley-Curtiss, 2010)
- social work practice roles within humane societies (Hoy, Delgado, Sloane, & Arkow, in press)

Through the efforts of many social workers—some named in this chapter and others who have innovated in practice and disseminated their work through social work curriculums, professional associations, supervision, and continuing education—inclusion of HAI within social work practice has come a long way since Bikales (1975) shared the tragic story of Mrs. F. and her dog, Lacey. For instance, the New York City Chapter of the NASW has formed a special interest group, Social Workers Advancing the Human-Animal Bond. This group "meets monthly to share information, discuss cases, listen to speakers, encourage advocacy, and support one another's efforts" related to HAI (NASW New York City Chapter, n.d., para. 1). Such mainstream inclusions of HAI within social work practice support well-being for both humans and animals, a goal we explore and celebrate in the subsequent chapters of this book.

3

Understanding Biological, Psychological, and Social Benefits of Human–Animal Interaction within a Strengths Perspective

In a study currently in progress on companion animals and well-being, a participant who was being interviewed named Donna (name changed to protect anonymity) simply stated, "I feel better. When I hold my cat, Rio, I just feel better." The benefits of animal presence, companionship, and interaction—be it through a brief interaction with a visiting therapy animal a person is meeting for the first time or a daily routine shared by a person and a cherished companion animal for years—may occur within biological, psychological, or social spheres of human functioning. In a review of 69 original, rigorously screened HAI studies, Beetz, Uvnäs-Moberg, Julius, and Kotrschal (2012) concluded that

> among the well-documented effects of HAI in humans of different ages, with and without special medical, or mental health conditions are benefits for: social attention, social behavior, interpersonal interactions, and mood; stress-related parameters such as cortisol, heart rate, and blood pressure; self-reported fear and anxiety; and mental and physical health, especially cardiovascular diseases. Limited evidence exists for positive effects of HAI on: reduction of stress-related parameters such as epinephrine and norepinephrine; improvement of immune system functioning and pain management; increased trustworthiness of and trust toward other persons; reduced aggression; enhanced empathy and improved learning. (para. 1)

Through the process of becoming aware of (and intentionally including) such benefits, social workers can begin to identify and engage with clients around their respective HAIs as strengths; these strengths can, in turn, be included in intervention plans to address client concerns and goals.

Such HAIs may also present as risks or liabilities. For instance, when an elderly dog who is the primary source of companionship for a person becomes ill and dies, that person may be at risk for a number of bereavement-related issues, which we discuss in depth in chapter 8, our chapter on loss of companion animals. We address the risks and liabilities of HAIs in chapter 4 of this book.

To limit our scope and focus to what is most salient to social work practice, for the bulk of this chapter, we discuss benefits of HAI that may occur through simply living with companion animals or through structured therapeutic interactions with animals. To provide readers with a strong empirical foundation for understanding how benefits related to HAI and the HAB may serve as strengths for clients within the scope of social work practice, we summarize and integrate relevant research related to the various types of benefits: physical (for example, reduced blood pressure and heart rate, increased oxytocin, potential for increased activity), social (direct—perceived social support from animal, indirect—animal as facilitator of increased interactions with other humans), emotional (for example, subjective feelings of attachment, comfort, reciprocal affection, amelioration of loneliness), and psychological (for example, experiencing increased self-efficacy and a sense of being needed, embracing the role or identity of an "animal person," being motivated to act, having a reduction in number or intensity of psychiatric symptoms). Some of these benefits may occur in the context of interacting with a therapy animal one has just met and may never see again, whereas others occur in the context of a long-standing, significant relationship with a companion animal who recognizes, knows, responds to, and is bonded with a person.

Understanding the Benefits of HAI:
A Biopsychosocial Perspective

Although we differentiated between HAI and HAB in chapter 1, we have not yet conceptually considered the word "benefit." Within the profession of social work, social workers have a responsibility to assess for and support the potential benefits of HAI and the HAB as they work with clients. In considering general definitions, *benefit* is defined by *Merriam-Webster's Online Dictionary* as "a good or helpful result or effect" ("Benefit," n.d.-b) and by *The Free Dictionary* as "something that promotes or enhances well-being; an advantage" ("Benefit," n.d.-a). Given such definitions, a benefit of an HAI or an HAB could thus be viewed as a strength within a client system. Social workers are trained to use an integrated biopsychosocial perspective to assess and understand the functioning of a given client system. In working with that client system, social workers explicitly focus on identifying existing and potential strengths and assets within the system that can be built on to address needs and goals; this view is known as the *strengths perspective*. Benefits (that is, strengths) related to HAI for humans can be delineated into three categories, although there is certainly overlap between them: benefits related to human physical health, benefits related to human psychological and emotional health, and social benefits (Morley & Fook, 2005; Smith, 2012).

How Do Animals Experience HAI and the HAB?

Little research has been done on how animals experience HAI and the HAB. Although researchers cannot interview animals and ask them directly, researchers can use species-specific physiological indicators and observed behaviors as proxies to understand HAI impact. Several studies explored physiological indicators and discovered that dogs experienced positive benefits during HAIs. Odendaal and Meintjes (2003), in studying positive interactions between humans and their dog companions, found that both species experienced significant decreases in blood pressure, along with significant increases in "feel-good" biochemicals such as endorphins, oxytocin, and dopamine. Bergamasco et al. (2010) similarly found that shelter dogs experienced reductions in heart rates and cortisol when interacting with shelter volunteers. In an exploratory study to determine changes in heart rate and other hormones within dogs and their humans during short-term interactions, both dog and human participants experienced increases in oxytocin and decreases in heart rate (Handlin et al., 2011). Handlin, Nilsson, Ejdebäck, Hydbring-Sandberg, and Uvnäs-Moberg (2012) explored psychological characteristics (from human perspectives) of dog–human relationships as being potentially related to physiological correlates; they reported that the more the humans kissed their respective dogs, the higher the oxytocin levels in both humans and dogs.

Combinations of observed behaviors and physiological proxies have also been used to explore how an animal may be experiencing HAI. Rehn, Lindholm, Keeling, and Forkman (2014) attempted to operationalize how dogs experienced their relationships with human owners through behaviors such as "changes in exploration, passive behaviour, independent play, social play, physical contact and tail wagging" (p. 65). Within their study, dogs whose human companions interacted with them more frequently showed more proximity-seeking behavior and less independent play behavior (Rehn, Lindholm, et al., 2014). In a study in which dogs were separated and then reunited with their respective humans,

> the mere return of the familiar person had a positive effect on oxytocin levels and induced contact-seeking behavior, whereas physical contact was necessary in order to induce a sustained increase in oxytocin levels and to decrease cortisol levels in the period following reunion. (Rehn, Handlin, Uvnäs-Moberg, & Keeling, 2014, p. 45)

Such findings, although limited to dogs, suggest that HAI can be experienced positively by animals and may convey similar physical benefits to the interacting human and animal. Anthropologist Samantha Hurn (2012), in her book *Humans and Other Animals: Cross-Cultural Perspectives on Human–Animal Interactions*, noted,

> Some pets certainly benefit from human hospitality and care. Others are not so lucky and appear to have been forced into 'pacts with the devil.' . . . Most pet animals are kept in isolation [from others of their own species], or in confined spaces, are reliant on their owners for the satisfaction of all their needs and often have to substitute the companionship of their own species for interactions with humans. For some species such as dogs, who readily accept humans as 'pack' members, this is less problematic than it is for other highly social, active or nervous animals who can be placed under considerable stress

if their human carers are unable to adequately meet their requirements. Rabbits, for example, have traditionally been housed in small cages and, while commonly kept as pets, do not always respond well to confinement and handling. However, the phenomenon of 'house rabbits' . . . where animals are given much greater freedom and the ability to socialize (albeit not necessarily with their own kind) leads to a much healthier and happier pet. (p. 110)

Benefits of HAI cannot be assumed to be conveyed to the animals involved in a given interaction, and species-specific needs must be accounted for to maximize potential benefits for a given animal. Additional, multispecies research is needed to more fully understand experiences of HAI and the HAB from the perspectives of various types of companion animals.

Physical Benefits of HAI and the HAB

The majority of research on human benefits of HAI focuses on physical benefits. Such benefits fall under three general categories: immediate and short-term health benefits, long-term benefits, and health promotion and protective factors. Of emerging interest are the interactive effects between these aspects, which several researchers and scholars are linking to the bonding hormone oxytocin (Beetz et al., 2012; Odendaal & Meintjes, 2003; Olmert, 2009). Immediate and short-term benefits are those that commence when experiencing HAI and cease shortly after the HAI ends. For instance, let us return to the participant mentioned at the beginning of this chapter, Donna, who stated, "When I hold my cat, Rio, I just feel better." Notice how Donna did not state exactly how she felt better. A substantive body of research offers some illumination as to what Donna was likely experiencing internally as she was holding and stroking her companion: Her blood pressure likely dropped (Allen, Blascovich, & Mendes, 2002; Allen, Blascovich, Tomaka, & Kelsey, 1991; Davis, 1991; Katcher, Friedmann, Beck, & Lynch, 1983; Manor, 1991; Slovenko, 1983), her heart and respiration rates likely also slowed (Allen et al., 1991, 2002; Manor, 1991), and oxytocin was released into both Donna's and Rio's bodies (Odendaal & Meintjes, 2003).

When Donna stops holding Rio and goes to work, these immediate short-term effects abate. On returning home, however, Donna picks up and holds Rio after being exposed to a stressful situation (such as a phone call from an angry family member who is upset about holiday plans). The immediate HAI short-term benefits would resume and serve to help mediate the physiological stress. This mediation effect explains anecdotal evidence of stress mediation and subsequent anxiety reduction as a result of HAI with a variety of populations. For instance, children testifying in court reportedly experience reduced anxiety when a court support dog is present (Dellinger, 2008; Holder, 2013), children reportedly experience reduced anxiety when a therapy dog is present (Prichard, 2012), and students from numerous universities anecdotally report stress reduction during HAI when therapy dogs are brought in during finals weeks (Christensen, 2013).

Emerging rigorous evidence also corroborates such stress mediation. An experimental study on the impact of the presence of a therapy dog on children's distress and cortisol levels during venipuncture found that children in the presence of a therapy dog demonstrated less distress and had lower cortisol levels (Vagnoli et al., 2015). In addition, a study found that salivary and heart rate indicators of physiological stress dropped significantly in children undergoing forensic interviews for alleged sexual abuse when a therapy dog was present (Krause-Parello & Friedmann, 2014).

Separating physical from psychological health benefits in HAI may thus be easier said than done, as there seems to be a complex physiological–psychological relationship at work. Beetz et al. (2012) suggested that the activation of the oxytocin system may explain such beneficial psychological and physiological effects of HAI, asserting, "As a common underlying mechanism, the activation of the oxytocin system does not only provide an explanation, but also allows an integrative view of the different effects of HAI" (p. 1). Clearly, oxytocin has a multifaceted and significant role underlying HAI benefits.

HAI's numerous long-term positive effects on health are also documented. Extensive empirical evidence links HAI to positive cardiovascular outcomes. Friedmann, Katcher, Lynch, and Thomas (1980) found a significant positive association between having pets and one-year survival after hospitalization for coronary heart issues. Because of continued accumulation of evidence over several decades, in 2013, the American

Heart Association (AHA) issued a scientific statement indicating that living with a companion animal, a dog in particular, was associated with decreased risk of cardiovascular disease and may have a causal role in reducing this risk (Levine et al., 2013). The AHA statement indicated that there were strong positive associations between lower systolic blood pressure and HAI, including one randomized control study (Levine et al., 2013). Table 3.1 summarizes the cardiovascular health factors identified within the AHA statement as being potentially positively affected by HAI.

Table 3.1: Summary of Cardiovascular-Related Health Factors Potentially Positively Affected by Human–Animal Interaction (HAI)

Health Factor	Potential HAI Impact
Blood pressure and hypertension	Decreased systolic blood pressure; lower heart resting rates; lower pulse pressure
Physical activity	Increased recreational walking (among those with dogs)
Cardiovascular reactivity to stress	Lowered blood pressure, lowered heart rate in response to mental stress
Survival rate	Increased likelihood of surviving one year after established cardiovascular disease

Source: Data are from "Pet Ownership and Cardiovascular Risk: A Scientific Statement from the American Heart Association," by G. N. Levine, K. Allen, L. T. Braun, H. E. Christian, E. Friedmann, K. A. Taubert, et al., 2013, *Circulation, 127*, pp. 2353–2363.

The complete AHA review of existing research on HAI, cardiovascular disease, and related risk factors, titled "Pet Ownership and Cardiovascular Risk: A Scientific Statement from the American Heart Association" (Levine et al., 2013), is available at no cost online in PDF form; see the reference for the link. HAI is also associated with improved plasma, cholesterol, and triglyceride values (Anderson, Reid, & Jennings, 1992; Rowan & Beck, 1994).

According to Fine and Beck (2010), recovery from illness includes many factors beyond mere biological processes, and beneficial relationships with animals are a positive influence on convalescence. A study by Staats, Wallace, and Anderson (2008) confirmed that a majority of people with companion animals believe their pets confer physical health benefits and cite this as a reason for choosing to live with them. This supports the assertion that having the responsibility of taking care of a companion animal can provide an incentive for people to take better care of their own health (Carmack, 1991). Even the mere observation of fish in an aquarium aids physiological indicators of relaxation to a measurable degree over observation of an unpopulated tank (Katcher et al., 1983).

Physical benefits of HAI have also been framed as generally protective of health overall, particularly with regard to living among companion animals. Cohabitation with companion animals has been linked to promoting physical activity (Manor, 1991; Rosenkoetter, 1991) and, as previously stated, is also significantly correlated with a higher rate of survival for patients one year after undergoing coronary surgery (Friedmann et al., 1980; Rowan & Beck, 1994). Adults who live with companion animals, as compared with those who do not, have fewer physician visits (Rowan & Beck, 1994; Siegel, 1990), experience fewer minor health problems (Serpell, 1991), incur fewer symptoms with psychogenic components, and use less medication (Akiyama, Holtzman, & Britz, 1987). Children who live with companion animals have been found to have stronger immune systems and fewer allergies as compared with children who live in pet-free homes (Fujimura et al., 2010; Gern et al., 2004). It is noteworthy that many of these longer-term benefits are specifically linked with living with companion animals over time—a factor suggestive of benefits unique to HAB.

Social Benefits of HAI and the HAB

The social benefits of HAI generally fall under two main types: *direct* (positive outcomes that occur directly through interaction or a relationship with the companion animal) or *indirect* (an increase in a person's positive prosocial interpersonal interactions as a result of the companion animal being a topic of mutual interest, that is, a *social conduit*; Prosser, Townsend, & Staiger, 2008; Wood, Giles-Corti, & Bulsara, 2005; Wood, Giles-Corti, Bulsara, & Bosch, 2007). With regard to direct social benefits, studies indicate that people experience an increase in perceived social support and decreased feelings of loneliness and isolation from a reciprocal, ongoing, and interactive relationship with an animal (Krause-Parello,

2012). Although most of these social benefits occur in the context of an ongoing relationship between a person and an animal (that is, an HAB), there is evidence that episodic visits with therapy animals may also increase social interactions among residents at institutions (Hall & Malpus, 2000).

Social benefits related to HAI can also occur within and across micro, mezzo, and macro client systems. Numerous research studies illuminate the social benefits related to HAI with micro client systems. For instance, two studies that comprehensively compared types of social support found that companion animals held numerous positive roles in the lives of children; children included companion animals in their family networks and ranked them highly (sometimes even highest) as confidantes and companions (McNicholas & Collis, 2001; Sable, 1995). Living with a companion animal can increase an adult's sense of perceived social support and decrease feelings of isolation and loneliness (Antonacopoulos & Pychyl, 2010). Companion animals may serve as playmates and travel buddies, and they can also provide continuity and companionship across one's social existence. In addition, people who are unmarried may benefit by having a range of roles they may engage in as part of their relationship with a companion animal (Cline, 2010).

Numerous studies demonstrate that people will interact more frequently and positively with a person who is accompanied by a dog compared with when that same individual appears without a dog. Examples of this phenomenon have been found both in vivo (Wood et al., 2005, 2007) and in hospital settings (Hall & Malplus, 2000; Marr et al., 2000). In everyday encounters, details of the person's apparel or the dog's collar and leash may have varied considerably, but people consistently spoke more frequently and positively to the person with the canine companion versus the person unaccompanied by a dog. According to the AHA's scientific review, individuals with dogs walk more than do individuals who do not have dogs (Levine et al., 2013). Dog walking as HAI serves a dual purpose and conveys both physical and social benefits. This illustrates that interactions are complexly intertwined, as are various other aspects of the biopsychosocial contexts in which client systems function (Zimolag & Krupa, 2010).

The social conduit effect goes beyond micro client systems; at the macro client system level, Wood et al. (2005) also demonstrated that increased community interactions among residents can be catalyzed through interactions at dog parks. Dog parks, contrary to the uninformed opinion, are not just for dogs. Rather, they are usually large, open, green spaces where people gather with dogs and watch them run and play off leash. There are unique norms in dog parks: Typically, one asks your dog's name but not yours—at least not initially. Simply put, people in dog parks connect around their enjoyment of their canine companions. It is not surprising, then, that dog parks are associated with increased community desirability among young highly educated professionals and are considered a community asset (Wood et al., 2005).

Emotional and Psychological Benefits

Both comfort (Zimolag & Krupa, 2010) and reciprocal affection (Odendaal & Meintjes, 2003) are perceived emotional benefits associated with HAI. In an exhaustive literature search for qualitative studies reporting in-depth findings relating to mental health–related benefits experienced as a result of living with a companion animal, Hoy (2014) identified three studies. All three studies used thematic analysis of data obtained through semi-structured individual interviews. In the first study ($N = 44$), three themes emerged: connectedness, emotional stability, and responsibility. In the second study ($N = 177$), four themes emerged: connectedness, empathy and therapy, self-efficacy, and pets as family. In the third study ($N = 4$), five themes emerged: belonging and connectedness, continuity, action and self-construction, participation, and acceptance. Connectedness emerged as the most frequent single theme across these studies. Responsibility, self-efficacy, and action and self-construction entailed similar content relating to caring for another dependent being; in combination, these themes were likewise represented across studies. Both responsibility and self-efficacy were evidenced by statements from individuals who reported wanting to commit suicide but refraining because they felt responsible for their companion animals. Results of a study by Zilcha-Mano, Mikulincer, and Shaver (2011) echo these themes and demonstrate that a companion animal acts as both a secure base and a safe haven that aids in coping successfully with life stressors. Additional studies have demonstrated that being a pet guardian offers a sense of identify and provides a legitimizing role for people (Zimolag & Krupa, 2010).

Benefits Related to Reducing Psychiatric Distress and Impairment in Individuals Living with Mental Illness

In addition to finding general HAI benefits related to emotional and psychological health, numerous studies have documented reductions in symptoms for specific subgroups of individuals with differing types of mental illness in different settings. Studies have demonstrated that a wide variety of factors are positively affected both by relationships with companion animals and through intentional animal-assisted therapy (AAT) interventions. Although such research is only beginning to reveal a vast untapped resource in HAI, the number of studies and the rigor with which research is being conducted are increasing.

In a study by Barker and Dawson (1998), the potential for decreasing anxiety among psychiatrically hospitalized patients through the implementation of loosely structured AAT group sessions was explored and found to significantly reduce symptoms for those with psychotic and mood disorders. Patients experiencing long-term psychiatric hospitalizations increased their verbal, nonverbal, and prosocial behaviors after visits with animals (Hall & Malpus, 2000; Marr et al., 2000). Yorke, Adams, and Coady (2008) uncovered the significant effects of equine-assisted therapy in helping riders overcome debilitating physical and psychological traumas.

The benefits available from companion animals for those with mental illnesses have also been investigated in the community setting. Interventions of this type are a good fit with the notion of providing services in the least restrictive environment as well as providing relationships that are easy to develop and maintain. Zimolag and Krupa (2010) showed that including a companion animal in the lives of those with serious persistent mental illness assisted in their ability to move beyond personal perceptions of stigma associated with their diagnoses by facilitating a greater sense of inclusion and integration with their communities as well as increasing their overall interaction with their immediate environment (Walsh, 2009a). Berget, Ekeberg, and Braastad (2008) found an increase in self-efficacy and coping abilities in participants with diagnoses of psychotic, affective, anxiety, and personality disorders after regular engagement in farm animal work sessions.

Raina, Waltner-Toews, Bonnett, Woodward, and Abernathy (1999) showed that elderly people's activities of daily living and overall well-being were supported and enhanced by companion animals. Similarly, elderly residents with cognitive impairments demonstrated reductions in their symptoms after a companion animal was added to the social milieu (Colombo, Buono, Smania, Raviola, & De Leo, 2006). A subpopulation of this group, those with Alzheimer's disease, have also been shown to benefit from animals that provide unconditional love in an institutional setting (Baun & McCabe, 2003). Citing potentially misleading conclusions (such as the effect the novelty of the introduction of animals into a given treatment regimen may cause) drawn from earlier studies, Hall and Malpus (2000) designed a methodologically rigorous experiment that demonstrated a significant increase in both nonverbal and verbal interactions among long-term elderly psychiatric patients.

Limitations of HAI Benefits and Other Considerations

Across areas of social work practice, "starting where the client is at" is cited as critically important in approaching practice; social work practice related to HAI is no different in this respect. HAIs and HABs are not one-size-fits-all phenomena. A person who does not like or fears specific species of animals is highly unlikely to experience benefits related to interaction with a member of that animal species. Rather, that person may actually experience adverse effects such as fear, anxiety, or discomfort. As with other aspects of social work assessment, it is essential that a social worker not assume or project beliefs and preferences related to HAI but rather explicitly explore such beliefs and preferences with a client when HAI is involved. People may prefer interactions with some species over others, and the experience of benefits may be mediated by such preferences; some individuals identify as being a "dog person" or a "cat person" to express such preferences. Preferences related to HAI (and subsequent potential benefits) are also culturally mediated; even within-species differences may account for cultural variability in which animals are considered to be appropriate companion animals. For instance, dogs of all shapes and sizes are widely recognized as companions in the United States, whereas in South Korea, midsized, yellow-furred dogs are considered food sources and are not appropriate as pets (Podberscek, 2009). The yellow Labrador retriever, described as the quintessential family dog and often used as a therapy dog in the United States, may thus elicit very different reactions depending on a person's origin and cultural norms. It is imperative that client preferences and beliefs related to animals be assessed and client choices to engage or not engage in HAI be honored.

Implications for Social Work Practice

Given the research evidence substantiating the biological, psychological, and social benefits of HAI and the HAB, it is clear that much could be missed by overlooking such potential client strengths and resources in social work practice. The companion animals that clients interact with or are bonded to may serve as significant strengths across the biological, psychological, and social spheres of clients' lives. The flexibility with which HAI interventions or the natural support afforded by living with a companion animal can be implemented or used is remarkable. Despite the accumulating recognition and demonstration of the physical, emotional, psychological, and social benefits available, this helpful aspect of companion animal relationships continues to go untapped. Given that many individuals likely reap benefits in many or even all of these domains when cohabiting with companion animals, omission of routine assessment for these is a startling practice gap.

Ethically, social workers are called to identify strengths within the unique aspects of clients' social and cultural diversity (NASW, 2015); recognizing and building on strengths within clients' social diversity related to HAIs and the HAB are within the scope of this ethical imperative. As social workers, we must recognize and respect existing and potential HAIs and HABs as legitimate aspects of our clients' social diversities. We often speak of "starting where the client is at" in social work, yet in failing to systematically inquire about clients' companion animals in our assessment processes, we may be excluding and invalidating what for some may be a primary or only source of social support and affection. According to Risley-Curtiss (2010),

> social work practitioners appear to have basic knowledge of the negative and positive relationships between humans and companion animals. About one-third are including questions about companion and other animals in their intake assessments, and a little less than 25 percent are including companion and other

animals in their intervention practice. The vast majority have had no special training or coursework to do so. (p. 38)

By having a basic familiarity with the biopsychosocial benefits of HAI and the HAB, social workers will be better able to identify and build on strengths when working with clients. Such identification begins with explicitly asking about the presence and importance of companion animals in clients' lives. In assessing individuals and families, social workers should routinely ask for information about clients' families and social support systems. Including questions about the presence of a companion animal or animals and the nature of the relationship with each animal in routine assessment allows HAI and the HAB—and related potential benefits—to be explicitly incorporated and built on as client strengths.

4

Risks and Ethical Issues Associated with Human–Animal Interaction

The benefits of HAI are numerous. Unfortunately, HAI and the HAB also entail potential risks and harms for both animals and humans. Such risks and harms may necessitate social work intervention or may raise ethical questions for social workers. In this chapter, we highlight some of these risks and harms within the context of social work practice by reviewing particular risks and liabilities for both companion animals and humans, delineating ethical concerns and legal responsibilities that social workers may encounter in HAI, and considering larger ethical questions regarding human–companion animal relations and the social work profession as initially raised in chapter 1.

Risks to Humans

Injuries, Zoonosis, and Allergies

Physical risks to people related to HAI can be divided into three categories: trauma or injury-related harm, *zoonosis* (disease or infection that is naturally transmissible from animals to humans), and human systemic reactions to aspects of an animal (for example, allergies). A cat scratch, as a body wound produced by sudden physical injury ("Trauma," n.d.), would fall under the category of injury or trauma; such injuries from interactions with companion animals may result from defensive or aggressive animal behavior or happen accidentally, such as when a frail older adult or child is knocked over by an exuberant large dog who is jumping up in play or friendly greeting.

As social workers, it is not within our scope of practice to provide medical treatment for such injuries. However, many physical injuries may be preventable if we provide human clients with education resources on how to safely interact with particular companion animal species. Knowledge of safe interaction with animals is also important for the personal safety of social workers engaged in community-based practice settings where they may encounter animals. It is squarely within the scope of social work practice to link human clients with care for animal-related injuries and with needed information and supports to interact safely with companion animals so that injuries can be prevented. Many companion animal rescue and advocacy groups offer free pamphlets or printable online information about how to safely handle cats, dogs, and other common companion animals. For instance, the American Veterinary Medical Association offers resources for micro educational approaches to dog bite prevention through parent education, as well as a detailed guide to macro community task force approaches (American Veterinary Medical Association, 2001). In addition to such written resources, local humane societies may offer other types of support; for instance, the Toledo Area Humane Society (TAHS) offers a free behavior helpline for individuals seeking assistance with a variety of different companion animal–related concerns. This service is offered to individuals irrespective of where they obtained the companion animal in question, and it can be accessed through an online form or a behavior hotline (TAHS, n.d.). In the event of a dog bite, the local animal control authority should be notified and proper medical treatment sought out. Animals who are ill or in pain are more likely to bite or scratch when handled; linkage to routine veterinary care resources can assist with detection and care for health issues that may put an animal at risk of uncharacteristically aggressive behavior. Some humane societies offer low-cost veterinary clinics; many large pet supply store chains also offer low-cost on-site veterinary services through having permanent in-store vet clinics or by hosting periodic veterinary clinics.

Routine veterinary care is crucial in the prevention and treatment of companion animal diseases that are communicable to humans; these diseases are called zoonotic diseases. The Centers for Disease Control and Prevention (CDC) provided the following three preventative tips for the general population with regard to zoonotic diseases: accessing regular veterinary care for companion animals; practicing good hygiene, such as hand washing after handling animals; and becoming knowledgeable about specific diseases that may be transmitted by particular animals (CDC, n.d.-b). As social workers seeking the most up-to-date, scientifically supported, and accessible information to support the health of our human clients and their companion animals, we have a wealth of resources at our fingertips through the CDC's user-friendly Web page, Healthy Pets Healthy People (CDC, n.d.-a). This CDC Web site provides an array of helpful information and tips related to the prevention of zoonotic diseases. Straightforward content about animal-specific conditions that can be transmitted to humans, as well as simple actions that can be taken to prevent them, is provided for backyard poultry, farm animals, reptiles and amphibians (with a separate section for turtles kept as pets), birds kept as pets, ferrets, small mammals, cats, fish, wildlife, dogs, and horses.

Although some people are at higher risk than others for zoonotic diseases, it is important to note that if proper precautions are taken, immunocompromised persons, pregnant women, and parents of young children often do not need to give up companion animals (CDC, n.d.-c). As social workers, we can link clients who are at particular risk of zoonotic diseases with the most up-to-date information and precautionary strategies so that they can make informed choices about their health and companion animals. Encouraging our clients to communicate their companion animal–related health concerns to their health care providers can similarly increase our clients' ability to make informed choices related to zoonotic health care concerns.

Human systemic reactions to animals are another area of HAI in which concerns about human health may jeopardize the place of a companion animal in a given household. People with oversensitive immune systems may react to proteins within an animal's urine, saliva, or dander; these reactions are termed *allergic reactions*, and the substances that are causing the reactions are referred to as *allergens*. Symptoms of an allergic reaction may range widely depending on the severity of the reaction, from itchy, watery eyes and running nose to life-threatening symptoms such as tongue swelling and throat closing (Asthma and Allergy Foundation of America, n.d.). Contrary to popular belief, pet hair is not an allergen, but it can collect allergens such as dander, urine, saliva, or dust. An allergy to a companion animal is diagnosed by a medical provider through symptoms, physical examination, medical history, and testing (usually in the form of blood work or a skin test).

If a person is allergic to a companion animal, a number of mitigating strategies may be used. The Asthma and Allergy Foundation of America (n.d.) makes the following recommendations: not sleeping with a pet, using a high-efficiency particulate arrestance (HEPA) air cleaner in the bedroom, opting for bare floors rather than carpeting whenever possible, wearing a dusk mask to vacuum, vacuuming with a HEPA filter, steam cleaning frequently, getting carpet with low pile, washing throw rugs in hot water, changing clothes after extensive exposure to an animal, covering bedroom vents with cheesecloth or other dense filtering materials, asking someone who is not allergic to the animal to brush the animal outside to remove dander, bathing the animal weekly, and talking to an allergist about medication and immunotherapy options.

As with other medical conditions related to companion animals, as social workers, our scope of practice precludes provision of medical treatment. However, it is well within our scope and practice to link clients with the best available information and resources on such medical conditions. We can also encourage our clients to communicate health care–related concerns with health care providers so that informed decisions about health can be made. Because we encounter animals during home visits and in the community, knowledge of animal behavior, zoonotic diseases, and animal-related allergy management can be important to our own self-care as well.

Emotional and Psychological Risks for Humans Engaged in Animal Caregiving: Compassion Fatigue and Secondary Trauma

In chapter 8 of this book, we explicitly consider human emotional and psychological risks associated with animal loss, as well as social worker responses to such. However, companion animal loss is not the only way in which humans may experience emotional and psychological risk associated with HAI. Excluding military personnel, those in protective service occupations—including police officers, firefighters, detectives, and animal rescue workers—were found to have the highest rate of on-the-job suicides between 2003 and 2010 (Tiesman et al., 2015). Results from the

CDC report titled "Prevalence of Risk Factors for Suicide Among Veterinarians—United States, 2014" indicated that veterinarians are more likely than the average member of the U.S. adult population to be diagnosed with psychiatric disorders, experience depression, and have suicidal ideations (Nett et al., 2015). The disproportionate prevalence of mental health concerns among those in animal caregiving occupations is linked with the following interrelated issues: compassion fatigue, secondary trauma, and burnout. Charles Figley, director of the Tulane Traumatology Institute, defined *compassion fatigue* simply as "emotional exhaustion, caused by the stress of caring for traumatized or suffering animals or people" (as quoted in Lizik, n.d., para. 4). Mehelich (2011) elaborated on compassion fatigue as follows:

> The "*double-edged sword*" phenomenon of working in the animal care industry—you've dedicated your life to making a positive difference for animals, but the emotional stress is draining, exhausting and taking a toll on you. You can't imagine doing anything else with your life, but outside of your work, do you have a life? You work in the animal care industry, not necessarily because you've chosen to, but because it's chosen you. You cannot exist without doing all that you can to care for and save animals. You love what you do, but the heartbreak and emotional strain on you is sometimes too much to bear. There is a term for all of this, it's called Compassion Fatigue (further referenced as CF) and it is normal, and very real.
>
> Not only does CF dominate your professional life, but it always rears its head in your personal life—sleepless nights, exhaustion, acute sadness, depression, isolation from friends, a life that feels out of balance, rides on emotional rollercoasters, and anger towards people in general for the terrible ways in which they treat animals. (pp. 1–2)

Individuals in animal caregiving occupations may be exposed to animals who have experienced horrific violence and abuse; through exposure to such animals and situations, these individuals may experience secondary trauma. *Secondary trauma* refers to a person being exposed indirectly to a traumatic incident involving the death, threat of death, serious injury, or bodily harm of a person or animal (Diaconescu, 2015).

Secondary trauma may result in acute stress disorder (lasting less than 30 days) or posttraumatic stress disorder (lasting more than 30 days); both disorders include symptoms such as intrusive images of the trauma, avoidance of things that remind one of the trauma, depersonalization or *derealization* (feeling disconnected from one's self or the context one is in), and overall difficulty in functioning (American Psychiatric Association, 2013). In contrast, *burnout,* a broader phenomenon not specific to helping professions, is a pervasive physical and emotional weariness that workers across workplace settings may feel when they repeatedly experience low workplace satisfaction, feelings of helplessness and being overwhelmed, little control over work, unrealistic requests, poor management or supervision, and a nonsupportive work environment (Mathieu, 2012).

Social workers must be sensitive to the risk factors experienced by those in animal caregiving occupations and encourage proactive self-care and healthy coping strategies among clients who work in such roles. Employee assistance programs may also be an appropriate linkage for those struggling with compassion fatigue and secondary trauma. Chapter 10 of this book details evolving specialized social work roles, including those within animal caregiving settings such as shelters and veterinary practices, in which services related to the prevention and treatment of compassion fatigue may be routinely provided. Assessing and linking to appropriate mental health supports and promoting self-care are crucial when working with individuals dealing with compassion fatigue and secondary trauma.

Financial and Legal Risks

Having a companion animal may also entail financial and legal risks. If the companion animal injures another person, the companion animal's owner may be held liable and sued. A barking dog may result in noise complaints; in a rental situation, this could put a person's housing at risk. Homeowners insurance often covers some liabilities related to financial and legal concerns for individuals who have companion animals and own homes. Coverage by policy varies widely, and some dog breeds may be excluded, so it is important to be knowledgeable about one's own policy coverage. Companion animals may also chew, scratch, urinate or defecate on, or otherwise damage property, resulting in monetary costs for the person responsible for the animal. Understanding and responding to species-specific needs regarding proper socialization and care, including environmental enrichment (for example, providing toys or other appropriate outlets for chewing, scratching, and other natural animal behaviors) and adequate exercise, can mitigate such risks. Social workers can link clients with local animal protection organization staff, who can provide consultation, education, and direction regarding these issues.

Veterinary care for animals who are ill may also result in large financial costs for clients; availability of resources to assist with such expenses vary widely by locality. Pet insurance is an option to help manage veterinary care costs; however, preexisting conditions are typically not covered, and pet insurance may not be affordable for many individuals. Just as social workers assist clients in locating other needed resources, they can assist clients in searching and applying for any available supports. The national organization RedRover does provide nationwide small grant assistance for urgent veterinary care; guidelines are available online at https://redrover.org/redrover-relief-grants. Many localities also offer low-cost spay, neuter, and vaccination services; local shelters and humane societies are typically knowledgeable about such local resources.

Risks to Animals

Animal Abuse and Neglect

Tragically, companion animals are vulnerable to and experience a wide range of harms in the context of HAI, commonly referred to as *animal cruelty*. (Other forms of physical harms and violence toward animals, such as institutionalized violence and culturally specific violence, are considered in more detail in chapter 6 of this book.) Some of the harms occur unintentionally, whereas others are deliberately inflicted on the animal. According to the Humane Society of the United States (n.d.), animal cruelty encompasses both intentional harmful or hurtful actions, such as beating, shooting, stabbing, or burning, and the failure to provide basic care, such as food, water, shelter, or veterinary care. *Animal abuse* typically refers to intentional acts of harm, whereas *animal neglect* describes failure to care for an animal; both can result in tremendous suffering or death for the affected animal. Animal neglect may occur as a result of lack of knowledge, lack of interest, or lack of resources. A widely accepted definition of animal abuse in the social sciences is "non-accidental, socially unacceptable behavior that causes pain, suffering or distress to and/or the death of the animal" (Ascione & Shapiro, 2009, p. 570).

According to the Humane Society of the United States (n.d.), the following are observable signs of animal cruelty: lack of veterinary care (evidenced by untreated wounds, scabs, emaciation, hair loss, and the like); inadequate shelter, particularly in extreme heat or cold; continuously tethered or chained dogs who endure social isolation and exposure; abandonment in former residences; and deliberate violence or harm, such as beating or attacking an animal. Situations in which many animals are kept together and neglected are referred to as *hoarding*; in such neglect instances, a wide, multiprofessional effort may be needed to intervene. Williams (2014) indicated that hoarding occurs when a number of animals are not being cared for, they are in an inappropriate environment, and the animals' basic needs are unmet or they are ill and not receiving veterinary treatment (p. 36). According to Steketee et al. (2011), the number of animals kept in a hoarding situation averages about 40 but may be 100 or more. The animals may urinate and defecate freely in the hoarding environment without any cleaning occurring, and the bodies of dead animals may not be removed from the premises, resulting in sanitation and health concerns for both humans and animals.

Human hoarding behavior may be gradual or sudden. Williams (2014) described the following types of hoarding situations: overwhelmed caregiving hoarding, in which the animals are passively acquired through failure to spay and neuter and there is a strong emotional attachment to the animals; rescuing or mission-driven hoarding, in which animals are actively acquired to prevent them from being euthanized; and exploitive hoarding, in which the humans actively acquire as many animals as possible to sell them for profit, while lacking any empathy for their well-being. Hoarders of all types often insist that the animals are happy and well cared for, despite evidence to the contrary. Tragically, at times, animals who survive hoarding conditions may be so damaged emotionally and physically that they must be euthanized (Berry, Patronek, & Lockwood, 2005).

Removing animals from hoarding situations provides relief for those individual animals who are affected but does not solve the problem: The hoarder is likely to again acquire animals and re-create the hoarding situation (Frost & Steketee, 2010). Moreover, after animals are removed from the premises, extensive damage and sanitation issues may need to be addressed for the human hoarder's well-being; the human hoarder may also need help to manage the grief or psychological distress resulting from the animals' removal. Both micro and macro social work skills may be needed to effectively intervene in an animal hoarding situation. Micro skills may be used by a social worker when providing therapeutically oriented treatment to humans struggling with hoarding behaviors or advocacy pertaining to facilitating removal of the animals and prosecution for animal cruelty. At the macro level, multisystem coalitions or task forces can be created to quickly and effectively provide an organized community response to the multifaceted issues presented in an animal hoarding situation. Examples of members of such a coalition include but are not limited to health department officials, cruelty investigators, mental health crisis responders, housing authorities, adult protective services, and child protective services. Hoarding-specific legislation can be passed, which creates a separate offense of animal hoarding that mandates psychological evaluation and prohibits future ownership of animals for those convicted of hoarding. Another resource is the Hoarding of Animals Research Consortium (Cummings School of Veterinary Medicine at Tufts University, n.d.), which offers assessment tools for dwellings and animal conditions, resources for therapists treating individuals who hoard animals, and guidelines for the creation of community response task forces on animal hoarding.

Animal Abuse and Neglect: Social Work Ethical and Legal Considerations

All states in the United States have laws prohibiting animal cruelty; however, it is incumbent on humans witnessing the cruelty to report it for such laws to be enforced. Social workers must consider both ethical and legal parameters involved in animal cruelty reporting: Although social workers have an obligation to maintain confidentiality toward their human clients, they also have the obligations of preventing harm to others and addressing social problems. The Ethical Principles section of the NASW *Code of Ethics*, under the value of Service, identified the primary goal of social workers as "to help people in need and to address social problems" (NASW, 2015). Individual needs are not prioritized above social problems; rather, both are listed as focuses to be addressed as part of the primary goal of social work practice. Animal cruelty has long been recognized as a social problem; child protection efforts emerged from animal protection efforts in the United States (Watkins, 1990), and the FBI (2016) has begun tracking incidents of animal cruelty alongside crimes such as arson, burglary, assault, and homicide. An FBI (2016) news story on the FBI's tracking of animal cruelty offenses stated,

> The National Sheriffs' Association's John Thompson urged people to shed the mindset that animal cruelty is a crime only against animals. "It's a crime against society," he said, urging all law enforcement agencies to participate in NIBRS [National Incident-Based Reporting System]. "By paying attention to [these crimes], we are benefiting all of society." (para. 11)

As stated in the Purpose of the NASW Code of Ethics section, "the *Code* offers a set of values, principles, and standards to guide decision making and conduct when ethical issues arise. It does not provide a set of rules that prescribe how social workers should act in all situations" (NASW, 2015, para. 9). Although social work ethical responsibilities toward animals are not explicitly named in the code, it does clearly indicate that social workers' ethical responsibilities extend beyond a prescriptive application of the code and that social workers' ethical responsibilities encompass efforts to ensure the well-being of the broader society. Social workers have an ethical responsibility to use their professional judgment and apply the values and principles espoused in the code to guide their decision making when dealing with emergent situations not explicitly noted in the code.

Ryan (2011) made a compelling case for future reform of the NASW *Code of Ethics* so that it is explicitly inclusive of considerations toward animals. However, the current NASW *Code of Ethics* is not written in a way that absolves social workers of any ethical responsibilities toward animal cruelty (or any other abusive situation that does not have an explicit reference in the code) in the interim. Several components of the code can be used to guide social work conduct in instances of animal abuse. Within the code, tensions inherent in social workers' dual obligations to individual clients and societal well-being are explicitly recognized; as stated in the Ethical Principles section under the value of Dignity and Worth of the Person, social workers are cognizant of their dual role to clients and the broader society. They seek to resolve conflicts between clients' interests and the broader society's interests in a socially responsible manner consistent with the values, ethical principles, and ethical standards of the profession. (NASW, 2015, Ethical Principles section)

Although promotion of societal well-being in and of itself is not an adequate rationale to violate confidentiality, section 1.01 of the NASW (2015) *Code of Ethics* offers additional insight, indicating that "social workers' responsibility to the larger society may on limited occasions supersede the loyalty owed clients." Section 1.02 explicitly states that "social workers may limit clients' right to self-determination when, in the social workers' professional judgment, clients' actions or potential actions pose a serious, foreseeable, and imminent risk to themselves or others" (NASW, 2015); it is worth noting that "others" is not explicitly limited to humans in section 1.02.

To prevent serious harm to companion animals related to animal abuse and neglect, a social worker may engage in a range of actions. Animals may be removed from the environment for their protection. However, as with removing at-risk children from homes, this is an intervention of last resort. In many cases, such as those involving unintentional neglect or harm, resources and education may be provided to alleviate the harm or potential harm done to the animal. Social workers encountering clients' animals who are neglected because of the clients' lack of resources can work collaboratively with humane society staff and cruelty investigators to assist human clients in linking to and accessing resources to meet the animals' basic needs, such as education to become aware of the animals' needs, pet food banks, low-cost or no-cost veterinary services, and assistance in providing dog or cat shelters for animals residing outdoors. Local humane societies and animal control officers are often able to direct social workers to such resources and can also assist in providing education and information about needed animal care.

In the event that one learns of an egregious act of deliberate cruelty toward an animal, the following steps are recommended by the Humane Society of the United States (n.d.): Make a report (call the police or 911 if you are not familiar with the locality's local animal cruelty investigating entity); document details such as date, time, and location as well as physical descriptions of all people and animals involved (cell phone photos and videos can be extremely helpful); and be willing to testify (most cruelty investigation entities will accept anonymous reports, but the likelihood of a successful outcome increases when a witness is willing to testify).

As noted in Shapiro and Henderson (2016), "there is, currently, no clear legal or profession-based protection for therapists who report prospective animal abuse" (p. 39). Given the lack of explicit professional social work guidelines in such instances, to both help preserve the therapeutic alliance and attempt to reduce the risk of legal and professional sanctions for breaking confidentiality to report past or threatened animal abuse, social workers need to be explicit about related confidentiality limits so that clients can provide informed consent for services. With regard to informed consent, Shapiro and Henderson (2016) suggested the following:

> As in all counseling, the therapist should spell out the limits of confidentiality at the beginning of treatment. This includes specifying what information the therapist may be obligated to present to other agencies such as the courts and the therapist's duty to warn regarding the danger to self or other humans. The issue of reporting prospective animal abuse should be discussed with the client and could issue in a signed agreement stipulating the therapist's intention to report such. (p. 39)

Shapiro and Henderson (2016) went on to express concern as to whether such an agreement would be legally or professionally binding. However, such a document does offer the spirit of informed consent in terms of delineating the extent and limitations of confidentiality. As stated in the Purpose of the NASW Code of Ethics section of the NASW (2015) *Code of Ethics,*

> there are many instances in social work where simple answers are not available to resolve complex ethical issues. Social workers should take into consideration all the values, principles, and standards in this *Code* that are relevant to any situation in which ethical judgment is warranted. Social workers' decisions and

actions should be consistent with the spirit as well as the letter of this *Code*. (NASW, 2015, para. 11)

If a statement explaining the limits of confidentiality pertaining to animal cruelty was incorporated into an agencywide policy, as well as in an informed consent document the client needed to sign, it may offer additional standing. As concluded by Shapiro and Henderson (2016), "clearly, we are in an area here where there is yet no satisfactory policy and therapists must make their own decisions" (p. 39).

To summarize, in ethically ambiguous situations, we are called as social workers to use the NASW *Code of Ethics* for guidance. Given that animal cruelty offenses are considered egregious enough to be tracked by the FBI along with other horrific crimes against society such as murder and assault, the social work profession needs to respond accordingly. As stated in the code, social workers have a dual role to clients and the broader society and are not relieved of ethical responsibilities in instances of animal cruelty. Rather, social workers need to resolve conflicts between human clients' interests and the interests of animals and the broader society in a manner consistent with the values and ethics of the profession (NASW, 2015). In some instances, referrals to and provision of education and resources can eliminate the harms experienced by companion animals at the hands of humans. However, in other instances, social workers need to take action to safeguard the well-being of vulnerable animals who are being or are about to be subjected to horrific cruelty. Failure to act in such situations is to be complicit in such cruelties, which have already been identified as crimes against society; social workers who are condoning deliberate animal cruelty through their failure to report or otherwise intervene to prevent it are not acting in a manner consistent with the spirit of the code.

Fortunately, some state legal statutes offer additional guidance on what to do when social workers occupying particular human service roles witness animal cruelty. Although veterinarians are the only profession currently mandated in 11 states to report animal cruelty (for ease of discussion, we refer to the District of Columbia in this paragraph as a state), numerous states require or permit individuals in specified human service roles (often held by social workers) to report animal cruelty, as detailed in Table 4.1. Three states (California, Maine, and Massachusetts) explicitly permit those in stated human service roles to report animal cruelty, whereas seven states (Connecticut, the District of Columbia, Illinois, Louisiana, Nebraska, Tennessee, and West Virginia) explicitly require those in stated human service roles to report animal cruelty. Three states (the District of Columbia, Massachusetts, and Nebraska) explicitly provide immunity for those in specified human service roles who report animal cruelty. Confidentiality related to those in human service roles who are reporting animal cruelty is explicitly addressed in three states (Louisiana, Maine, and Tennessee). It is crucial that social workers familiarize themselves with animal cruelty reporting laws in their state that are relevant for those in specified human service roles.

Table 4.1: Animal Cruelty Reporting Requirements for Human Service Workers in States Where Such Reporting Is Mandated or Permitted

State	Reporting Requirements
California	Provides that any employee of a county child or adult protective services agency, while acting in his or her professional capacity or within the scope of his or her employment, who has knowledge of or observes an animal whom he or she knows or reasonably suspects has been the victim of cruelty, abuse, or neglect, **may report** the known or reasonably suspected animal cruelty, abuse, or neglect to the entity or entities that investigate reports of animal cruelty, abuse, and neglect in that county.
Connecticut	An employee of the Department of Children and Families who, in the course of his or her employment, has reasonable cause to suspect that an animal is being or has been harmed, neglected, or treated cruelly **is required to make a written report** to the commissioner of agriculture.
District of Columbia	Provides that any law enforcement or child or protective services employee who knows of or has reasonable cause to suspect an animal has been the victim of cruelty, abandonment, or neglect or observes an animal at the home of a person reasonably suspected of child, adult, or animal abuse **shall provide** a report within two business days to the mayor. If the health and welfare of the animal is in immediate danger, the report shall be made within six hours. No individual who in good faith reports a reasonable suspicion of abuse shall be liable in any civil or criminal action.

State	Reporting Requirements
Illinois	Provides that investigation specialists, intact family specialists, and placement specialists employed by the Department of Children and Family Services who reasonably believe that an animal observed by them when in their professional or official capacity is being abused or neglected in violation of the Humane Care for Animals Act **must immediately make a written or oral report** to the Department of Agriculture's Bureau of Animal Health and Welfare. However, the Department of Children and Family Services may not discipline an investigation specialist, an intact family specialist, or a placement specialist for failing to make such a report if the specialist determines that making the report would interfere with the performance of his or her child welfare protection duties.
Louisiana	**Requires reporting** by any state or local law enforcement officer or any employee of government or of a government contractor who in his or her professional capacity routinely investigates alleged abuse or neglect or sexual abuse of a child or abuse or neglect of an adult who becomes aware of evidence of neglect or abuse of an animal. No person required to report shall knowingly and willfully obstruct the procedures for receiving and investigating a report of abuse or neglect or shall disclose, without authorization, confidential information that was reported. No person shall make a report knowing that any information therein is false.
Maine	Provides that health care professional and other social service employees **may report** a reasonable suspicion of animal cruelty, abuse, or neglect to the local animal control officer or to the animal welfare program of the Department of Agriculture, Food and Rural Resources. The reporter shall disclose only such limited confidential information as is necessary for the local animal control officer or animal welfare program employee to identify the animal's location and status and the owner's name and address.
Massachusetts	Provides that during any investigation or evaluation, any employee of the Department of Children and Families or person employed pursuant to a contract with the department, when acting in his or her professional capacity or within the scope of his or her employment, who has knowledge of or observes an animal whom he or she knows or reasonably suspects has been the victim of animal cruelty, abuse, or neglect, **may report** the known or suspected animal cruelty, abuse, or neglect to the entities that investigate reports of animal cruelty, abuse, or neglect or any local animal control authority. No person making such a report shall be liable in any civil or criminal action

(Continued)

State	Reporting Requirements
Massachusetts *(continued)*	by reason of such report if it was made in good faith. Nothing shall impose a duty on the department to investigate known or reasonably suspected animal cruelty, abuse, or neglect. Nothing shall prevent the department, area office, or subdivision from entering into an agreement, contract, or memorandum of understanding with the entities that investigate reports of animal cruelty, abuse, or neglect to require such reports or to engage in training in identification and reporting of animal abuse, cruelty, and neglect.
Nebraska	Provides that any employee of a governmental agency dealing with child or adult protective services, animal control, or animal abuse, while acting in his or her professional capacity or within the scope of his or her employment, who observes or is involved in an incident that leads the employee to reasonably suspect that an animal has been abandoned, cruelly neglected, or cruelly mistreated **shall report** such to the entity or entities that investigate such reports in that jurisdiction. Nothing shall be construed to impose a duty to investigate observed or reasonably suspected animal abandonment, cruel neglect, or cruel mistreatment. Any person making a report is immune from liability except for false statements of fact made with malicious intent.
Tennessee	Provides that any state, county, or municipal employee of a child or adult protective services agency, while acting in a professional capacity or within the scope of employment, who has knowledge of or observes an animal that the person knows or reasonably suspects has been the victim of cruelty, abuse, or neglect, **shall report** the known or reasonably suspected animal cruelty, abuse, or neglect to the entity or entities that investigate reports of animal cruelty, abuse, and neglect in that county. Nothing shall be construed to impose a duty to investigate known or reasonably suspected animal cruelty, abuse, or neglect. Nothing shall expand or limit confidentiality requirements under existing law relative to child or adult protective services. The name of any employee of a child or adult protective services agency who reports known or reasonably suspected animal cruelty, abuse, or neglect shall remain confidential.

State	Reporting Requirements
West Virginia	Provides that, whenever a law enforcement officer, pursuant to a response to an alleged incident of domestic violence, forms a reasonable suspicion that an animal is a victim of cruel or inhumane treatment, he or she **shall report** the suspicion and the grounds therefor to the county humane officer within 24 hours of the response to the alleged incident of domestic violence. Also provides that, in the event a child protective service worker, in response to a mandated report, forms a reasonable suspicion that an animal is the victim of cruel or inhumane treatment, he or she **shall report** the suspicion and the basis therefor to the county humane officer within 24 hours of the response to the report.

Note: Language pertaining to whether reporting is required (mandated) or permitted has been put in bold for ease of observation. In states where statutes indicate that reporting is permitted (for example, "may report") rather than required (for example, "shall report"), permission is generally meant to indicate that a person making such a report shall be not liable in any civil or criminal action by reason of such report if it was made in good faith.

Source: Adapted from "Cross-Reporting of Animal and Child Abuse," by American Veterinary Medical Association, 2014 (https://www.avma.org/Advocacy/StateAndLocal/Pages/sr-animal-abuse-cross-re-porting.aspx?PF=1).

Although some egregious animal cruelty scenarios warrant aggressive prosecution, other scenarios may be optimally resolved through education, additional support services, and other resources; it is beyond the scope of professional social work practice to make such animal welfare–related determinations. As professionals with expertise in assessing, investigating, and resolving instances of animal cruelty, animal cruelty investigators can make such determinations. Social workers who encounter animal cruelty in their work can use principles from the NASW *Code of Ethics*, as well as any legal mandates, as a guide while working with cruelty investigators and clients, with the ultimate goals of minimizing harms and maximizing safety for both the humans and the animals involved.

Stress and Fatigue among Animals in Therapeutic Roles

Unfortunately, risks to animals related to HAI are not limited to abuse and neglect; animals who are very well cared for and who hold therapeutic roles may be vulnerable to fatigue, injury, and other stresses and strains related to their roles (Serpell, Coppinger, Fine, & Peralta, 2010). For instance, therapy animals who reside in residential settings may have limited or no time away from humans seeking attention and affection from them. Animals used in individual therapy as cotherapists may or may not have their quality-of-life interests adequately addressed. To reduce the risk of negative impact on animals in therapeutic roles, social workers doing animal-assisted interventions must have knowledge of animal behavior, particularly stress and anxiety behaviors that are specific to particular species as well as individual animals.

According to John Brown (personal communication, June 30, 2016), certified professional dog trainer–knowledge and skills assessed, Animal Behavior College certified dog trainer, owner of Let's Train Dog Training, and trainer of psychiatric service dogs for veterans who have posttraumatic stress disorder, behavioral signs that a dog is stressed may include but are not limited to

- stress panting (differentiated from heat panting by lips being pulled back and cheeks being wrinkled during panting)
- whining
- barking
- tucking tail between legs
- holding ears back
- exhibiting disinterest in interaction
- excessive water drinking
- high speed wagging of the tail tip (versus whole-tail wagging)
- excessive licking of the body
- licking lips
- ignoring commands that are typically followed
- avoiding eye contact
- refusing treats
- leaving sweaty paw prints
- exhibiting lower body posture or lowered head
- exhibiting clingy behavior toward the handler

When such stress behaviors are observed in a therapy dog doing therapeutic work, the social worker should end the therapeutic interaction and allow the dog time to relax. Proactive measures, such as limited-time interactions during visits and provision of a quiet space for resident therapy dogs so they can take a break from interactions, should be used to help prevent such stress. Resources on specific standards and ethical codes for the various therapeutic roles held by animals are provided in chapter 9 of this book. Social workers have an obligation to ensure the well-being of animals who are therapeutically assisting them in their practice.

Risks Related to Anthropocentrism

Companion animals may also be at risk for stress and fatigue if demands placed on them are not consistent with their species-specific abilities. In his book *The New Work of Dogs: Tending to Life, Love, and Family*, Katz (2004) conceptualized the work of companion animals kept as pets in contemporary U.S. society as being to meet various emotional and social needs—which may or may not be realistic, given an animal's species, temperament, capabilities, and so on—of their human companions. Katz (2004) noted that *anthropomorphizing*—projecting human traits onto nonhuman animals who may or may not encompass such traits—and placing unreasonable emotional and social expectations on companion animals can set them up to be viewed as companionship failures who are subsequently abandoned either emotionally (for example, not interacted with or shown affection or interest) or in actuality (turned loose or taken to a shelter) by their human caregivers. Each species of animal, as well as individual animals within a given species, have particular social and emotional needs that may be partially or completely ignored if they are viewed and treated as human surrogates rather than as unique nonhuman beings who may encompass some human traits but who also are distinctly nonhuman.

The social work ethical value of appreciation of diversity may have utility when considering differences in needs and behaviors across species in the context of HAI. Much like ethnocentrism is a barrier in multicultural relationships, anthropocentrism may foreclose on one's abilities to connect with and enjoy mutually beneficial relationships with other species. Having healthy and realistic expectations of relationships with companion animals can be important for human clients to maximally benefit from such relationships. Reevy and Delgado (2014) found a relationship between neuroticism and affection toward one's companion animal with animal caregivers; in some circumstances, strong attachment to animals can actually be correlated with poor human interpersonal functioning. Although companion animals may be expected to act as such to varying degrees, they are not humans; rather, they offer a unique relationship and a type of interspecies connection and interaction that can benefit humans and animals alike.

Conclusion

HAI and the HAB entail both benefits and risks for animals and humans. The observation of such risks may necessitate direct social work intervention, such as referrals to education or financial resources, or may necessitate collaboration with animal protection professions to safeguard the well-being of both humans and animals involved in a given scenario. Social workers may not be able to prevent such risks; however, social workers can be proactively aware of and responsive to harms associated with HAI and thereby can reduce distress and suffering for both humans and animals.

5

Companion Animals within Family Systems across the Life Course

In social work practice with clients and their family systems, a client's own definition of "family" is typically honored and used to the extent possible within the constraints of an existing agency service system. "Family" may be considered to include family of origin and extended blood relatives, spouses or partners, children, and other supportive individuals. As stated in chapter 1, over half of the households in the United States (for example, 65 percent of households according to the APPA, 2015, National Pet Owners Survey) reported having at least one companion animal; the majority of the responding households indicated that they considered their companion animals to be family members. Although there is some variation, such sentiments are echoed across sociodemographic groups.

In 2006, Risley-Curtiss and colleagues interviewed a sample of women who identified as women of color to explore how they described their experiences and views about their companion animals. When asked if they considered their companion animals to be family members, 13 of the 15 women interviewed indicated that they did:

> Many women who explained the family nature of the relationship used such terms as *child, our boys, brother, baby,* or *grandchild* when talking about their pets. For example, Patty said, "I like to spoil my dog, and I don't treat my dog [like] he's just an animal. I treat him like part of our family. He's my baby, you know . . . I treat him as part of me." Roz, on the other hand, explained the family nature of the relationship in terms of her pet's devotion to people: "She was . . . very much so a member of the family, and it was so wonderful. Like when you came home from being

59

tired and so stressed out from work, and there would be Sparkles greeting you at the door, smiling and so happy to see you." (Risley-Curtiss, Holley, Cruickshank, et al., 2006, p. 436)

Among a sample of adults with mental illness living alone (that is, without other people), the respondents cited the importance of a cat as a valued companion who did not replace human companionship but, rather, offered a unique and valued form of companionship specific to human–cat interaction:

> I really don't have any friends, like I mentioned, but on the plus, at least, I'm happy to hear somebody [the cat] playing with their toys. . . . And I'm happy in the fact that when I'm on my computer, all of a sudden I have someone who "sticks their butt in my face" so that they have attention, and I'm more than happy to give them that attention. . . . And I'm glad to have someone watching out for me as well, 'cause they like to sit up in their cat tower, 'cause of the fact that cats love to be up in high areas. . . . And the fact that I learned about other cat behaviors, like when the cat's staring at you, that's also a sign of affection . . . and other things, besides rubbing and playful biting. I've learned a lot, to tell you the truth . . . I overall feel happier in the fact that it's nice to have someone around that thinks of me, you know. I mean that's something I don't have in my life right now . . . I just don't have anyone [human] really in my life that's you know special to me that thinks of me. . . . At least I have a little someone who's fuzzy and is on four legs that thinks of me, and that at least makes me feel good. (Hoy, 2016, p. 12)

Companion animals have also been named as survivors in obituaries. When this occurs, they are typically listed along with human family members, and terms of endearment are often used to describe the companion animals (Wilson, Netting, Turner, & Olsen, 2013).

Despite the importance of companion animals within clients' family and support systems—as a potential strength or area of concern—such relationships are largely overlooked in social work assessment and intervention (Risley-Curtiss, 2010). Among the wide variety of theories that seek to explain the lifespan development of humans (as well as the ways in which people define "family"), Bowlby's attachment theory; Carter,

McGoldrick, and Carter's model of the family life cycle; and Merton's variation on role theory provide useful lenses through which to view people's lives as dynamic, evolving processes that encompass HAI and the HAB in meaningful ways. Within this chapter, we use these theoretical frameworks to explain the relevance of considering companion animals within client family and support systems, and we offer explicit related dimensions to consider for assessment and intervention across the lifespan. To limit scope and focus, we reference companion animals; however, it is important to keep in mind that species of animals treated as companions and considered family can vary within and across cultures (Hurn, 2012).

Companion Animals and Attachment across the Life Course

Attachment to animals, as well as the developmental impact of HAI, is underpinned by neurobiological and genetic processes pertaining to human functioning. In *The Social Neuroscience of Human–Animal Interaction* (Freund, McCune, Esposito, Gee, & McCardle, 2016), the biological basis of the HAB is explained in detail. The relevance of neurobiology and oxytocin for attachment and bonding with animals is summarized by Julius, Beetz, Kotrschal, Turner, and Uvnäs-Moberg (2012) as follows:

> The possibility of establishing a human-animal bond—or any enduring bond—rests upon brain features and functions derived from our remote, common ancestry with dogs. We share the phylogenetically very ancient network of loci in the fore- and midbrain that generate hormones and regulate social behavior and responses to stress. . . . In addition, we appear to share with our pets the neuropeptide oxytocin, which may be thought of as the essential "lubricant" for social bonds of all types—between parents and offspring, between mating and other social partners, and between humans and their pets. Oxytocin has receptors through the central nervous system, and it serves key social functions (in addition to its role in labor and breast feeding). These include facilitating proximity to and social interaction with various partners, reducing anxiety and inducing calm, and

increasing pain thresholds. Notably, oxytocin is released in both humans and animals as a consequence of stroking, skin-to-skin contact, and, possibly, shared gaze. (p. vi)

In an editorial review of research, Hollander (2013) concluded that a deficit of oxytocin, the hormone associated with bonding and attachment, is related to anxiety and social impairments; as detailed in chapter 3 of this book, the potential benefits (and even protective factors) of endogenous oxytocin release resulting from bonding with and attachment to companion animals may lie easily (yet still relatively untapped) within reach of social work practitioners as well as their clients.

Attachments in infancy, as well as throughout the human life cycle, are rooted in neurobehavioral processes (Julius et al., 2012). Attachment theory, as first posited by psychoanalyst John Bowlby in the 1960s, generally focuses on human relationships, humans' ability to form trusting bonds, and the ways people react to and behave within a social system when faced with stressors (Bowlby, 2005). Bowlby (2005) indicated that proximity to (and the specificity of) other individuals and behavioral responsiveness were necessary components in forming secure attachments. Patterns of secure attachment established early in life extend into adulthood and inform an individual's definition of family as well as an ability to function and relate effectively with others. Therefore, expansion of attachment theory to include the integration of companion animals into the understanding of the human lifespan, family roles, and functioning is a reasonable conceptual leap to make in understanding the long presence companion animals have held in human lives—sharing food, living space, and affection.

Children must form secure attachments with parents to form a base from which to thrive socially. An underrecognized attachment figure can readily be found, however, in a family's companion animal, traditionally a dog or cat. A human attachment figure's absence or inability to provide emotional input can be supplemented by animal family members—or, alternately, mirror adequate sources of it, thus strengthening already positive attachment bonds with family members (Tipper, 2011). Julius et al. (2012) considered how HABs differ from human–human bonds and may even have potential benefits that human–human bonds do not; they suggested that because companion animals are adapted for behavioral reciprocity and relationships but do not have the complex cognitions and needs of humans, HABs can provide a different kind of secure base within a relationship that can be psychologically transformative for humans.

As they proceed from childhood to adulthood, people take on the responsibility of creating and facilitating attachments of bonding for the succeeding generations. Companion animals can serve to make new attachment figures for adults regardless of previous experience with animals in childhood. Although there are some cross-cultural differences (Risley-Curtiss, Holley, & Wolf, 2006), these bonds are generally shown to be relevant in a wide range of household environments: the single adult, a cohabiting partnership, or any arrangement of blended family with or without children (Bikales, 1975; Faver & Cavazos, 2008; Flynn, 2000; Putney, 2013, 2014). Companion animal bonds and attachment remain relevant as people begin to enter their elder years. Animals provide consistent nonjudgmental companionship and unconditional love in the lives of those who may be at risk for becoming increasingly isolated. Companion animals also provide a source of engagement with members of younger generations who may be reluctant to interact with older family members. The presence of companion animals is a conduit to community cohesion when individuals' social networks are disrupted by transitions to residential care facilities (Prosser et al., 2008). Putney (2014) found that a relationship with a companion animal also had an impact on the overall psychological well-being of older lesbian adults, a group that experiences social marginalization to a more acute degree than their heteronormative counterparts do. However, not all attachments to companion animals produce purely positive outcomes. Chur-Hansen et al. (2010) warned that elderly adults may be at high risk for hyperattachment and overreliance on their companion animals, which leads to greater dysfunction instead of beneficial support. In the face of dwindling social interaction, elderly people can feel the loss of pets especially severely; we explicitly consider the loss of animals and practice implications within chapter 8 of this book.

Roles of Companion Animals within Family Life Cycles

As interactive members of human family systems, companion animals may hold particular roles that transform as the systems evolve over time. The model of the family life cycle as initially conceptualized by Carter and McGoldrick (1988) details an evolution of eight stages that individuals move through when meeting specific tasks created by their family environments: family of origin experiences, leaving home, premarriage stage, childless couple stage, family with young children, family with adolescents, launching children, and later family life. Many of these tasks involve challenges presented by shifting relationships with other family members that occur throughout the lifespan. McGoldrick, Preto, and Carter (2015) have greatly expanded this initial nuclear family–centric model to encompass the wide range of diversity within and across family structures that people may experience. Role theory posits that individuals seek and fulfill specific contextual functions in their ongoing interactions with other people. Roles are guided by social norms and generally serve a mutually beneficial purpose for families and society at large. With their inclusion in family systems, companion animals may fill roles to varying degrees. These roles may be unique to the companion animal or may be roles that are unmet by other people (because of either their absence or their inability) but can be met to varying degrees by the companion animal. We do not suggest companion animals should be assessed and intervened with as surrogate humans but, rather, they should be understood on their own auspices as unique beings within a given family system who may have meaning, value, and varying roles within that system.

Within an abbreviated model of the nuclear family–centric life cycle initially articulated by Carter and McGoldrick (1988), Turner (2005) delineated numerous roles of animals that can be helpful to social workers in illuminating the importance of a companion animal with a given client system. Although Turner framed these companion animal roles within a nuclear family life cycle, such roles and functions may be identified and relevant within a wide variety of family compositions. Companion animal roles across a family life cycle are described by Turner (2005) as follows:

- **Stage 1: Unattached Young Adult:** In this stage, the young adult is developing a life of his or her own, apart from the family of origin; companion animal attachment can be very strong; the animal often holds the role of roommate, confidante, and/or best friend as someone the person can spend time with and who greets them at the door with unconditional love; the animal can help alleviate isolation or loneliness the young adult may be experiencing. (pp. 12–13)

- **Stage 2: Newly Married Couple:** In this stage, two adults are coming together and creating a family of their own; companion animal attachment can be very strong; the animal may hold the role of a child and be referred to as babies or kids, particularly among families without human children. (p. 13)

- **Stage 3: Family with Young Children:** In this stage, the couple begins having human children, and the role of the companion animal may change; adults may have less time to spend with the animal due to the demands of young children, and the adults' attachment to the companion animal may decrease; children in the family begin developing relationships with the animal, and the animal may hold a peer-like, best friend or sibling role for the child/children. (p. 14)

- **Stage 4: Family with Adolescents:** In this stage, children are developing autonomy from parents; families may acquire companion animals during this time because of perceived import of role of animals in lives of children; animal roles with adolescent(s) may be particularly salient as a confidante and help to alleviate loneliness and support associated with individuating. (p. 15)

- **Stage 5: Launching Children and Moving On:** During this stage, sometimes referred to as the "empty nest", adult children may be leaving the home; in households where parents are still married, the parents are rediscovering each other; the parents may be experiencing a loss of their role as caregiver to human children, and animals may provide an opportunity to care and nurture; attachment to animals may be high. (pp. 15–16)

- **Stage 6: Families in Later Life:** During this last stage, the family faces many changes and potentially stressful events that must be adjusted to such as retirement, death of spouse, physical health changes and relocation; the role of an animal as companion along with the physical and emotional benefits associated with human-animal interaction may be particularly salient; older adults may also be concerned about who will care for their animal in the event of death or incapacitation. (p. 17)

The presence of companion animals in such roles can oftentimes smooth such transitions and aid in overall family cohesion. As stated above, at different points in a family life cycle, the roles of companion animals and human attachment to them may vary. On the basis of empirical research, Albert and Bulcroft (1988) concluded that among adults, "pets can be an important source of affection and attachment among divorced, never-married, and widowed people, childless couples, newlyweds, and empty-nesters" (p. 550). Some adults reported receiving emotional comfort from their dogs nearly as often as they did from their romantic partners (Kurdek, 2009). Among children, McNicholas and Collis (2001) found in a study of children's natural support systems that companion animals even outranked certain adults in their capacity to serve as confidants and facilitators of emotional release (see also Rew, 2000), supporting self-esteem and other tasks of social adjustment.

The influence of HAI and the HAB on children can also be understood in terms of how such effects relate to cognitive, social, and emotional development. Self-esteem and a positive social orientation are examples of social–emotional development; learning to read, write, and do math are examples of a child's cognitive development (Endenburg & van Lith, 2011). The findings of a 2011 review conducted by Endenburg and van Lith on how companion animals influenced childhood development can be summarized as follows:

- HABs may influence child emotional development through increasing self-esteem, increasing autonomy, increasing empathy, and providing emotional support.
- HABs may influence child social development through increasing social competence, enhancing social interactions, increasing empathy, and strengthening social networks.
- HABs may influence child cognitive development through facilitating language acquisition, enhancing verbal skills, and serving as a motivator for learning and the acquisition of knowledge.

In many of the studies reviewed by Endenburg and van Lith (2011), merely having an animal was not sufficient to see developmental benefits; it was the child's bond with the animal that was found to be particularly salient. Endenburg and van Lith (2011) cautioned that it was difficult to claim a causal effect, as there may be significant differences between families with and without companion animals and HABs:

> The 'social climate' in families with companion animals may be different to that in families without companion animals. This makes the causal effects of parenting style on the development of children difficult to disentangle from the contribution made by companion animals. (p. 212)

That said, HAI and the HAB clearly have the potential to have a positive impact on childhood development. Social workers need to proactively identify and incorporate such tools within their work with children and families, building on them as existing natural strengths and supports within clients' social systems. HAI and the HAB can also be linked with negative aspects of family interactions, including abuse and violence. In chapter 6 of this book, we explicitly consider the interconnections between violence toward animals and violence toward people, including interconnections within family systems.

Companion Animals in Family and Client Systems: Implications for Practice

For social workers to identify the import and impact of companion animals within client's lives, the social work adage of "starting where the client is at" can be operationalized by asking clients about their animals and experiences with animals. When assessing an individual or family, social workers typically ask questions that identify family members and household composition. Such sections within an assessment form a natural space in which to inquire about the presence of companion animals and the nature of the human–animal relationship. It is important to ask explicitly about companion animals. As explained by Sable (1995),

> showing interest in the animal allows for discussion of issues such as euthanasia or loss of a pet that may arise during treatment or may actually be a precipitating reason for seeking help. Unless it is clearly permitted, clients may be reluctant or embarrassed to reveal how important their pets are to them. (p. 338)

Possible questions that can be incorporated into family, household, or social support sections of assessments include but are certainly not limited to the following:

- Do you have any animals? If yes, please describe (name, species, age, how long had).
- How important is your animal(s) to you?
- How would you describe your relationship with your animal(s)?
- Do you feel your animal(s) help or benefit you? If so, how?
- Do you have any concerns, fears, or stress related to your animal(s)? If yes, please describe.

The above questions identify specific, potentially salient aspects of HAI within a family system (including a family unit defined as a human and a companion animal). The first question identifies the presence or absence of a companion animal within a given client system. The second question assesses the extent to which a person may be attached or bonded to a given animal, and the third question allows for elaboration on the value and meaning of the animal's presence for a given client. The last two questions allow for explicit identification of the relationship with the companion animal as a strength that can be incorporated into treatment and for potential stressors and concerns related to the animal that may need to be addressed within treatment planning and intervention.

With regard to intervention strategies to address companion animal–related concerns that may emerge in response to the above questions, the Mayor's Alliance for NYC's Animals (a coalition of animal rescue and human service groups) created a tool kit specifically to assist social workers and other human service professionals in incorporating HAIs within their work. This tool kit is titled Helping Pets and People in Crisis and can be viewed online at http://www.helpingpetsandpeoplenyc.org/; much of the information is geared toward practitioners in New York City but can be modified or serve as a starting point for social workers in other communities. The tool kit includes strategies for responding to domestic violence, homelessness, human hospitalization and illness, animal hoarding, pet relinquishment, and animal-assisted therapy. Although we address these concerns in more detail throughout this book, this Web site serves as an easily accessible online resource for practice reference. To help ensure companion animals are recognized as being important to a given client or family, the online tool kit includes a sample pet informa-tion page that can be included with a client chart, as shown in Figure 5.1 and viewable online (Mayor's Alliance for NYC's Animals, 2015).

Figure 5.1: Sample Pet Information Page

Pet Information			
Name of Pet:			
Length of Time Owned:			
Species:	Breed:	Age:	Gender:
Color Pattern:		Weight:	
Additional Description:			
Veterinarian Name:			
Veterinarian Number:			
Recent Annual Vaccination Dates:			
Is pet spayed or neuted? ☐ Yes ☐ No If yes, when:			
Pet Behavior Checklist			
Friendly ☐	Anxious/Nervous ☐	Scared ☐	
Aggressive ☐	Guarding Animal ☐	Fearful ☐	
Bites ☐	Barks (dogs) ☐	Declawed (cats) ☐	
House Trained ☐	Indoor only ☐	Good with cats/dogs ☐	
Hides ☐ If so, where?		Other:	
Where is the pet originally from?			
Does the pet have a special diet? What is the pet's diet?			
Contact Information			
Emergency Contact Name:			
Emergency Contact Telephone Number:			
Additional Emergency Plan:			
Owner Name:			
Owner Telephone Number:			

Given that many clients consider animals to be family or otherwise vitally important parts of their lives, it is important that consideration of companion animals be embedded and institutionalized within social work practices, paper forms, and electronic chart fields. Explicitly incorporating content about clients' companion animals within assessments and information gathering enables social workers to proactively address concerns about companion animals and identify strengths related to HAIs. Such inclusion of companion animal consideration also honors the potential social diversity within clients' lives by recognizing their meaningful relationships with companion animals rather than systematically dismissing the possibility of such relationships by omitting related content in social work forms and questions.

6

The Link between Violence toward Humans and Violence toward Animals

As social workers, we may encounter violence toward animals through working with clients who have deliberately beaten or hurt animals or who are themselves fleeing abusive relationships in which their companion animals are also targets of abuse. In the context of HAI within given family systems (as discussed in chapter 5 of this book), both humans and animals may be abused. Typically, when considering violence toward animals in terms of relevance for social work practice, what situations come to mind are

> instances in which an individual has harmed, often publically and without justification, a single animal or perhaps a group of animals. . . . [What] we rarely think about is how prevalent violence to animals is in our own society. . . . Violence toward animals is truly universal—it is found in every culture and in every time period. (DeMello, 2012, p. 237)

We focus the bulk of this chapter on how social workers can better respond to such violence in the context of their work with human clients. However, human-perpetrated violence toward animals takes many forms. Because we are writing with an emphasis on relevance for social work—a values-driven profession that explicitly encompasses environmental and macro contextual factors—we would be remiss to not at least acknowledge and consider the wider societal context of human violence toward animals.

The separation of purposes animals serve into discrete categories (and respective roles) within a given society creates the contextual background for what does and does not constitute abuse or maltreatment. Animal mistreatment in the food production system is not only tolerated but often framed as an expected functional aspect, whereas the same manner of mistreatment of a companion animal in a residence is construed as abuse and punishable by law. Cultural context further exemplifies this disconnect—for example, dogs currently inhabit roles both as food and as companions in South Korea (Podberscek, 2009). Socially sanctioned foundations for violent and abusive interactions between human and nonhuman beings are vast and well-established, and they may vary greatly between age groups and cultures (Faver, 2013). For instance, the food, clothing, entertainment, research, and pet industries all have, to varying extents, socially sanctioned modes of operation in which violence may be systematically inflicted on animals. Such system-embedded and sanctioned violence toward animals can be considered a form of "institutionalized violence" (DeMello, 2012) and is largely excluded from current designations of animal cruelty. There is also culture-specific violence toward animals that, although not built into various social institutions, may be culturally acceptable to at least some members of a given population; "for instance, bullfighting in Spain, foxhunting in England, and cockfighting in rural America are examples of violent activities toward animals that . . . are seen as culturally acceptable—at least by a certain segment" (DeMello, 2012, p. 240).

In contrast, *deviant violence* refers to acts of violence toward animals that are generally considered to be unacceptable by a given society; such acts are often illegal (DeMello, 2012). This form of violence toward animals is what is typically considered to be animal abuse or animal cruelty. A widely accepted definition of animal abuse within the social sciences related to HAI is "non-accidental, socially unacceptable behavior that causes pain, suffering or distress to and/or the death of the animal" (Ascione & Shapiro, 2009, p. 570). An in-depth examination and critique of institutionalized, mass-scale violence toward animals is beyond the scope of this book; Ryan's 2011 book *Animals and Social Work: A Moral Introduction* offers a compelling moral and conceptual framework for social work consideration of and responses to institutionalized violence toward animals. Rather than attempt to duplicate aspects of his seminal work, we encourage readers to read and reflect on Ryan's (2011) call for reforms broadening social work ethical and moral responsibilities related to such violence.

The purpose of this chapter is to help equip social workers to identify and respond to the deviant type of violence toward animals, commonly understood to be animal abuse. Such animal abuse often occurs concurrently with other forms of interpersonal violence, such as intimate partner violence (IPV) and child abuse; this concurrence is referred to as "the link" between violence toward animals and violence toward people (Ascione & Arkow, 1999). Within this chapter, we address assessments and interventions related to aspects of the link, with emphasis on connections within family systems.

Connections between Violence toward Humans and Violence toward Animals

Animal Abuse within the Contexts of Family and IPV

In a study of 38 women living in a domestic violence shelter, among the 28 women who reported having companion animals, 71 percent reported that their partners had threatened their animals and 57 percent reported that their animals had been hurt or killed by their partners (Ascione, 1997). Another study of women in shelters indicated that at least half of the participants reported that their partners had threatened or harmed their companion animals (Flynn, 2011); women who reported that their companion animals have been abused were also more likely to have experienced more frequent and severe violence from their abusers than women whose companion animals were not abused (Ascione et al., 2007; Fitzgerald, 2007). Although the bulk of research focuses on male-perpetrated IPV, it is important to keep in mind that women also perpetrate IPV toward nonviolent partners (Archer, 2000). In this chapter, we discuss animal abuse in the context of IPV, also referred to as *domestic violence*, in terms of existing research, which focuses heavily on male perpetrators and female survivors. However, because women also perpetrate animal abuse in the context of IPV, social workers need to be mindful of and responsive to such situations.

The function of violence toward companion animals in the context of IPV varies considerably. Displacement of aggression onto the animal; harming or threatening to harm the animal as a coercion, an intimidation, or a control tactic; and harming or threatening to harm the animal to directly or indirectly punish a person who cares about the animal are all possible functions of animal abuse within a family system (Faver & Strand, 2007). Failure to take into account the HAB in the context of IPV can result in individuals remaining in life-threatening situations: Because they are afraid of companion animals being harmed, survivors may delay leaving or choose not to seek safe shelter elsewhere because they do not wish to leave their animals behind (Faver & Strand, 2003a, 2003b; Fitzgerald, 2007). Abuse of and threats toward companion animals in the context of IPV serve as a form of emotional abuse of the people who are bonded to the abused or threatened animals (Arkow, 2014; Faver & Strand, 2007). Such abuses and threatened abuses of companion animals may cause psychological trauma to the women (Faver & Strand, 2007) and children (McDonald, Ascione, Williams, & Brown, 2014) exposed to them.

In reviewing and summarizing research related to animal abuse in the context of IPV, Faver and Strand (2007) underscored the following cross-study findings as particularly important in understanding of how companion animal abuse can function as a powerful and devastating form of emotional abuse:

- It is common for batterers to harm their partner's pets as a control strategy. Control strategies include but are not limited to demonstrating or confirming power, forcing participation in the abuse, perpetuating a context of terror, teaching submission, preventing leaving, punishing leaving, isolating the partner, and expressing rage.
- Many battered women consider their companion animals an important source of emotional support, and this seems to be especially true among battered women whose pets are abused.
- Battered women care about the safety of their pets both within abusive relationships and after coming to domestic violence shelters.
- Concern for the safety of companion animals affects women's decision making about staying with or leaving an abusive partner.
- Women's self-reports indicate that their batterer's abuse of their pets has a direct, immediate emotional impact.

- The children of battered women often witness the batterer's pet abuse and may experience emotional distress; some attempt to protect pets, whereas others may imitate the abuse.

As social workers, we can use the preceding findings highlighted by Faver and Strand (2007) as guideposts for potentially important areas of assessment and intervention in working with survivors of IPV.

Social Work Responses to Animal Abuse in the Context of IPV

In assessing individuals with IPV, it is crucial that social workers ask about the presence of companion animals and any concerns that an individual may have about such animals. A simple question such as "Do you currently have any pets?" enables the social worker to establish that an animal is present in the household. Faver and Strand (2007, p. 64) suggested the following questions, derived from their review of related research: "Has an animal you care about ever been hurt?" (Jorgenson & Maloney, 1999, as cited in Faver & Strand, 2007) and "Does concern over your pet affect your decision making about staying with or leaving your partner?" (Ascione, 2000a, as cited in Faver & Strand, 2007).

To explicitly assess how animal abuse manifests in the context of IPV, we adapted the following questions from the Duluth Model Power and Control Wheel (initially modified by Safe Passage, an agency that serves domestic violence survivors, as cited in Arkow, 2014, pp. 9–10):

- **Coercion and Threats:** Has your partner threatened to harm or kill your pet if you leave or assert any independence?
- **Emotional Abuse:** Has your partner called your pet names, or given away your pet, or killed a pet to take away your primary source of comfort and unconditional love?
- **Intimidation:** Has your partner harmed or killed a pet and threatened that the same thing will happen to you if you don't comply with the abuser's demands?
- **Minimizing, Denying, Blaming:** Has your partner blamed you or the pet's behavior as necessitating the cruelty to the animal? Killed a pet and then said it doesn't matter because the animal was old?

- **Legal Abuse:** Has your partner tried to take possession of a pet for which you have been the primary caretaker? Filed or threatened to file charges of pet theft against you if you leave with the pet?
- **Isolation:** Has your partner refused to let you take your pet out to the vet? Prohibited you from you from allowing your dogs to socialize with other dogs?
- **Economic Abuse:** Has your partner refused to allow you to spend money on adequate pet food or veterinary care? Has your partner done so and then blamed you when the neglect is noticed by authorities?
- **Using Children:** Has your partner harmed or killed a pet to intimidate your children? Blamed the death or disappearance of a family pet on you to create a wedge between you and your children?

After ascertaining the specific nature of companion animal concerns within a given client's experience of IPV, social workers can then work with clients to formulate intervention strategies that explicitly address such concerns. In working with individuals who are dealing with animal abuse in the context of IPV, the Helping People and Pets in Crisis tool kit resources for domestic violence (Mayor's Alliance for NYC's Animals, n.d.) can be very useful. This tool kit contains resources for developing a pet safety plan, a pet go bag, and tips on advocating for a pet to be included in an order of protection. Routinely including companion animals in safety planning may entail both making logistical plans (establishing where to go and when) and taking such preemptive measures as ensuring "all pet care documentation—licenses, microchips, vaccinations, veterinary bills, registration papers, receipts, etc.—are in the survivor's names so as to avoid complicated custody disputes" (Arkow, 2014, p. 12).

Mezzo and macro level social work strategies are often necessary to advocate for and develop resources to address identified housing needs related to companion animal abuse within the context of IPV. For instance, on completing a statewide survey of domestic violence shelters in California, Komorsky and Woods (2015) advocated for greater community awareness and support of companion animals' importance to IPV survivors to help remedy a critical service gap that was identified: Although more than 75 percent of shelters surveyed in their report asked questions about shelter entrants' relationships with companion animals, none of the shelters' services offered accommodation for companion animals. Arkow (2014) similarly found that

> a study by the Ohio Domestic Violence Network reported that 79% of responding shelters see this [safe housing services for pets] as a critical issue. . . . Unfortunately, only 14% of responding shelters offered safe housing services for pets and only 25% routinely included information about pet safety in their written materials. (p. 10)

Safe housing programs for companion animals may entail the construction of animal housing at domestic violence shelters. The advantage of this is that the entire family fleeing abuse (including the companion animal) is kept intact (Arkow, 2014); however, it requires significant funding and time resources. Social workers interested in establishing on-site housing for companion animals at domestic violence shelters can apply for Domestic Violence Safe Housing grants offered by a national nonprofit known as RedRover; applications can be accessed online at https://www.redrover.org/node/1099. RedRover also offers a start-up manual for on-site companion animal housing at domestic violence shelters (Phillips, 2012); this manual includes explicit guidance on issues related to policies and procedure development.

Off-site safe housing for companion animals can be developed through partnerships with veterinary clinics, boarding facilities, or humane societies. For instance, the TAHS has partnered with the local domestic violence hotline to create the Safe Place Program. Through this program, TAHS places the animals of those going into domestic violence shelters in temporary foster homes. The establishment of such a partnership does not require the start-up funds of on-site housing for companion animals at domestic violence shelters, but it does necessitate separating the companion animal from the rest of the family who is fleeing abuse. Such partnerships do alleviate the need for a person leaving an abusive situation to have to choose between his or her safety and leaving a companion animal behind or giving the animal up. In the event that such a partnership has not yet been established, social workers or other shelter staff can apply on behalf of a person to obtain a Domestic Violence Safe Escape Grant through RedRover; these grants pay for temporary boarding or veterinary care to enable people leaving domestic violence to move their companion animals to a safe location. Domestic Violence Safe Escape Grant applications can be obtained online at https://www.redrover.org/node/1108.

At the policy level, social workers need to advocate for domestic violence definitions that explicitly recognize animal cruelty as a dimension of domestic violence and for inclusion of companion animals in domestic violence orders of protection. According to Arkow (2014), seven states (Arizona, Colorado, Indiana, Maine, Nebraska, Nevada, and Tennessee) have revised their legal definitions of domestic violence to "include acts of cruelty, abuse or neglect against animals that are intended to coerce, control, punish, intimidate, terrorize, exact revenge, or commit other emotional harm upon an intimate partner" (p. 11). States are also including animals as eligible victims within protection orders; according to Arkow (2014), "27 states, Puerto Rico, and the District of Columbia have enacted statutory authority specifically granting courts the power to include companion animals and/or livestock in domestic violence orders of protection" (p. 11).

The development of community partnerships between various agencies and stakeholders involved in antiviolence efforts—including human service providers and animal protection agencies—is crucial to developing both policy reforms and the needed community resources to assist people with companion animals who are experiencing domestic violence. As described by Arkow (2014), such efforts may take the form of

> statewide and local coalitions; inclusion of animal care and control agencies in multi-disciplinary teams; identification of pet-friendly transitional housing; therapy animal visits to domestic violence shelters; low-cost pet food; veterinary and spay/neuter services; emergency pet sheltering; cross-reporting protocols; and other innovative ideas. (p. 11)

Additional information about and resources for such coalition-building innovations can be obtained at the National Link Coalition Web site at http://nationallinkcoalition.org/.

Emotional distress and trauma reactions related to animal abuse in the context of IPV must also be assessed for and addressed in both adults and children who have been exposed to it. McDonald et al. (2014) found that children's exposure to animal abuse in the context of IPV may be more predictive of trauma, anxiety, and depression symptoms than proximity of exposure toward violence between human partners. Again, explicitly asking questions such as "Did you witness or were you exposed to your animal being harmed?" and "How did you react?" enables social workers to assess for trauma and other mental health concerns such as anxiety or depression. In the event that mental health–related concerns are identified, referrals to or provision of trauma-informed mental health care is essential.

Animal Abuse and Elder Abuse

Animal abuse may also occur in the context of elder abuse. A summarization of findings from a national survey of Adult Protective Services (APS) supervisors conducted by the Humane Society of the United States and the National Center on Elder Abuse indicated the following concerns:

- More than 35% of respondents reported that clients seen by APS talk about pets having been threatened, injured, killed, or denied care by [a] caregiver.
- More than 45% reported that they have encountered evidence of intentional abuse or neglect of animals when visiting clients.
- More than 92% said that APS workers encountered animal neglect coexisting with a client's inability to care for himself/herself, indicating that reports of animal neglect may be an important warning sign for the presence of self-neglect by vulnerable adults.
- More than 75% of respondents noted that clients' concerns for their pet's welfare affected decisions about interventions or additional services. Many people indicated that their clients often refused services or housing if the needs of their pets were not taken into consideration. However, few agencies had established working relationships with the appropriate animal care and control agencies in their area.
- Despite these concerns, only about 35% indicated that their agency includes questions about a client's animals on intake/assessment, fewer than 25% have policies in place for reporting suspected animal cruelty and only 19% have formal or informal cross-reporting and/or cross-training with animal agencies. (Lockwood, 2002, p. 10)

More recently, Peak, Ascione, and Doney (2012) conducted a national survey of state-operated adult protection services and found that efforts to assess and address the connection between elder abuse and animal cruelty remain inconsistent and underdeveloped. Including questions about animals in assessments with older adults is crucial if social workers are to identify and respond to potential needs and concerns. Ascione and Peak, in collaboration with the Utah Division of Aging and Adult Services Directors (which includes APS), developed a draft protocol that can be used in both initial screening and evaluation and investigation; the protocol is modeled after one developed by Ascione for use in domestic violence situations (Ascione & Peak, 2009). Examples of their suggested questions include

- How many pets or other animals do you care for?
- How does having a pet or caring for another animal help you?
- How do you care for your pet or other animals?
- Do you have concerns about the health and welfare of your pet or other animal?
- Do you have concerns about your ability to care for your pet or other animal?
- Do you have concerns about what will happen to your pet or other animals if you are no longer able to care for them?
- Has anyone ever harmed your pet or other animals? (Ascione & Peak, 2009)

By routinely and explicitly asking such questions, social workers can proactively identify and address animal-related issues affecting client well-being, such as those exemplified by the 1975 Bikales case study.

Understanding and Responding to People Who Abuse Animals

As stated earlier, witnessing violence against or attempting to protect a companion animal is traumatizing for children. In addition, it may serve as behavioral modeling for perpetuating acts of violence toward animals, a phenomenon excruciatingly detailed in a series of 18th century engravings by Hogarth titled *The Four Stages of Cruelty* (DeMello, 2012). Longitudinal research conducted by Tapia (Rigdon & Tapia, 1977; Tapia, 1971) initially linked childhood perpetration of animal abuse with other types of aggressive and antisocial behaviors, and subsequent research (Ascione, 1993; Ascione & Shapiro, 2009) has continued to support such a connection. Lunghofer (2016a, 2016b) indicated that childhood animal abuse is likely to co-occur with adverse childhood events, which may also need assessment and intervention. First incorporated into the DSM-III-R in 1987, children's abusive behavior toward animals remains a criterion for conduct disorder in the DSM-5 (American Psychiatric Association, 2013). Abusive behavior toward animals in childhood is also correlated with a predisposition to meeting criteria for antisocial personality disorder in adulthood (Risley-Curtiss, 2013; Vaughn et al., 2009; Walsh, 2009b; Zilney & Zilney, 2005). Whether perpetrated by children or adults, abuse toward animals is a serious concern and needs to be addressed. Safety for both the animals and the people involved is paramount; chapter 4 in this book explicitly addresses ethical and legal considerations related to reporting animal abuse.

With regard to increasing social worker awareness of and responsiveness to children who have abused animals or witnessed animal abuse, Lunghofer (2016a) suggested the following acronym to guide practice: ROAR—*r*ecognize signs of abuse, *o*bserve interactions with animals and caregiver responses, *a*sk about animals, and *r*efer for services if the child has abused animals or witnessed abuse. The Childhood Trust Survey on Animal-Related Experiences (Boat, 2014) offers screening questions for children, adolescents, and adults. Examples of questions from the survey include the following:

- Have you or your family ever had any pets?
- Do you have a pet or pets now?
- Has your pet ever been hurt? What happened? Have you ever felt afraid for your pet or worried about bad things happening to your pet? Describe.
- Have you ever seen someone hurt an animal or pet? What happened? Have you ever seen an organized dog fight? How old were you? Tell me about it.
- Have you ever hurt an animal or pet? How old were you? Tell me about it. What kind of animal? Were you alone when you did this? Did anyone know you did this? What happened afterwards? (Boat, 2014, pp. 1–2)

Animal abuse is a multifaceted phenomenon. Once current or historical animal abuse is identified through screening questions such as those provided in the Childhood Trust Survey on Animal-Related Experiences, additional assessment is necessary to guide appropriate intervention responses. Animals and Society Human-Animal Interaction director Dr. Lisa Lunghofer indicated that the following dimensions of animal abuse are important to assess. Although these dimensions were recommended for assessment with children, they may also prove useful when assessing adult perpetrators of animal abuse:

- **Severity:** Degree of injury, frequency, duration, number of species
- **Culpability:** Degree of planning, acting alone versus with others; having to overcome obstacles in order to carry out the abuse
- **Motivation:** Curiosity, fear of the animal, peer pressure, pleasure from inflicting pain, sexual arousal related to the animal
- **Attitudes and Beliefs:** Awareness/unawareness of the needs of animals, cultural practices related to animals, ways to discipline animals
- **Emotional Intelligence:** Level of empathy, ability to express feelings, ability to form relationships with others
- **Family History:** Physical/sexual abuse, domestic violence, neglect, exposure to animal abuse
- **Mitigating Circumstances:** Accepts responsibility, feelings of remorse, able to form bonds with animals (Lunghofer, 2016b)

Exploration of the above dimensions will allow for a more nuanced understanding of occurrences of animal abuse and planning of or linkage to interventions that address identified areas of concern.

Examples of existing evidence-informed practices that explicitly target animal abuse include AniCare for adults (Shapiro & Henderson, 2016), AniCare Child (Shapiro, Randour, Krinsk, & Wolf, 2014), and Children and Animals Together (CAT) Assessment and Intervention Program (Risley-Curtiss, 2014). We identify these practices as evidence informed rather than evidence based because although there is not yet extensive research on these approaches, each draws on evidence-based components of related interventions for trauma and antisocial behaviors. The AniCare and AniCare Child books are not manualized practices; rather, these books function essentially as tool kits from which one can draw guidance, depending on the particular needs of the client (Lunghofer, 2016b). AniCare for adults offers interventions that help with establishing the working relationship with the client, establishing accountability, developing empathy as an interpersonal skill, developing other interpersonal skills such as respect and nurturance, and using other complementary approaches such as problem-solving therapy, trauma-focused therapy, and narrative therapy (Shapiro & Henderson, 2016).

AniCare Child, as explained by Lunghofer (2016b), focuses on three objectives: development of empathy, development of self-management skills, and development of a sense of accountability. To reinforce what is addressed in therapy, parental or caregiver involvement—if there is such a supportive presence in the child's life—is also a crucial component of AniCare Child (Lunghofer, 2016b). A cognitive behavioral perspective undergirds AniCare Child techniques, which focus on the interrelationships between children's attitudes toward animals, beliefs about animals, and behavior with animals (Lunghofer, 2016b). Examples of AniCare Child techniques are discussion, exercises, and projective activities such as puppets, play, and drawing; interaction with live animals may or may not be included, depending on the supervision available, the ability of the child to self-regulate, and the type and size of the animal (Lunghofer, 2016b). As with any interaction with live animals, the safety of both the child and the animal are paramount, and depending on the nature of the animal abuse, such an interaction may be contraindicated. Specific areas focused on with such techniques include problem solving, frustration management, attitude and belief restructuring about animals and violence, empathy development, emotion management, attachment issues, and accountability (Lunghofer, 2016b).

CAT is a psychoeducational group intervention developed and provided by Dr. Risley-Curtiss and the Arizona School of Social Work, in collaboration with the Arizona Animal Welfare League and Society for the Prevention of Cruelty to Animals (AAWL):

> CAT's intervention and treatment philosophy is guided by ecological systems theory, a major tenet of social work practice. Rather than utilize a purely psychological framework to focus on the diagnosis of an individual child or youth, the

"person-in-environment" approach of social work practice emphasizes the ways in which children and families live in and interact with their environments. Thus, each child who is referred to CAT receives an in-home assessment from a Master-level social worker, the core component of CAT's holistic approach to intervention. In addition, at least one caregiver, and siblings if appropriate, are required to attend the CAT sessions along with the client child. (Risley-Curtiss, 2014, para. 6)

A total of 14 sessions, each lasting one to one and a half hours, are held at the AAWL in Phoenix (Lunghofer, 2016b). CAT is not designed as a therapy but rather as an adjunct to other therapeutic services (Risley-Curtiss, 2014). CAT groups focus on

the development of prosocial skills: responding to the feelings of others; responding to anger, fear, and peer pressure; helping others including animals; and understanding animal needs and behavior. Activities include prosocial modeling, working with therapy dogs, making things for the animals at the shelter, inter-acting with and caring for shelter cats and kittens, and weekly homework. (Risley-Curtiss, 2014, para. 7)

Other psychosocial education programs, such as the Chicago-based Lifetime Bonds (Safe Humane Chicago, n.d.), focus on preventing animal abuse by targeting youth at risk of abusing. Through Lifetime Bonds, boys in custody learn how to train dogs, a skill that can serve as an asset when reentering the community as well as facilitate the development of prosocial behaviors (Lunghofer, 2016b).

New methods of assessing and treating animal abuse continue to be developed. More than 31 states have enacted laws permitting or mandating psychological assessments or counseling for those convicted of animal cruelty; "such programs, conducted by trained therapists, can be integrated with batterer intervention and counseling programs to better address the elements common to both crimes" (Arkow, 2014, p. 12). Additional information about such ongoing efforts can be found at the National Link Coalition Web site, http://nationallinkcoalition.org/. Webinars on assessment of and intervention for childhood animal abuse, along with other aspects of the link between violence toward animals and violence toward people, are offered free of charge through a partnership between Animals and Society Institute and the Humane Society Academy (Lunghofer, 2016a, 2016b).

The Importance of Interprofessional Collaboration in Addressing the Link

Just as in other social work practice settings, effective partnering with professionals from other disciplines is essential in effectively working with client systems that include companion animals; such partnering is especially crucial when violence is involved. Many of the programs and coalitions referred to in this chapter emerged from collaborations between social workers, animal protection staff, law enforcement professionals, legal professionals, veterinary professionals, and many others. Arkow, Boyden, and Patterson-Kane (2011) introduced an extremely detailed handbook to guide veterinary staff in ethical responses to animal mistreatment. In it, they encourage coalition between veterinary and social work practitioners. Law enforcement may similarly use social workers' firsthand observations in forensic analyses conducted during investigations of animal abuse. Support from social workers may also assist those working with animals, such as in cases of compassion fatigue experienced by animal shelter and veterinary staff. Finally, social workers may be experts who can inform the legal decision-making process by educating and thereby influencing lawmaking and judiciary decisions.

Concluding Thoughts

Violence toward companion animals may be an indicator of other forms of abuse in the household or psychopathology, and it is also increasingly recognized as a crime against the broader society (FBI, 2016). At the micro practice level, social workers need to be inclusive of companion animals in their assessment of and interventions with client systems affected by interpersonal violence. Often, mezzo level practice skills may also be needed to help establish interprofessional collaborations and resources for clients and their companion animals. At the macro practice level, social workers need to advocate for laws and policies that are inclusive of companion animals who are part of family systems affected by violence.

The social work profession also must continue to grapple with larger ethical issues related to violence toward animals. Matsuoka and Sorenson (2013) and Faver (2013) argued for the reconfiguration of basic social welfare conceptualizations (and, by extension, social work practice) to integrate concerns regarding nonhuman animals on the premise that the balance of interspecies interdependence is threatened when institutionalized violence against companion animals is tolerated. An example of this integrated approach is found in Ontario, Canada, where recognition of this connection resulted in Guelph County Family and Children's Services and its Humane Society being reunited some 80 years after they had split into separate organizations (Zilney & Zilney, 2005). This move toward interagency cohesiveness reflects the idea many individuals hold—that, as one respondent in a qualitative study reported, stewardship over the environment (and all of the creatures in it) is a "duty inherent to being human" (Putney, 2013, p. 65). How and to what extent such stewardship—for example, responsibilities to safeguard the environment and nonhuman animals—fits within the profession of social work is a question that will continue to be raised.

7

Animal Companionship and Human Diversity

Humans have kept animals as companions or pets for millennia in various types of societies worldwide. Dogs were domesticated at least 15,000 years ago for hunting assistance and, by also providing companionship, were likely the first pets (DeMello, 2012). Although animals exist in nature irrespective of humans, the notion of "companion animal" is socially constructed and historically and culturally contingent. As explained by DeMello (2012),

> once incorporated into human social worlds, they [animals] are assigned to human categories, often based on their use to humans, and it is these categories (lab animal, pet, and livestock) that shape not only how the animals are seen, but also how they are used and treated. (p. 10)

Although many people around the world currently keep companion animals, attitudes toward animals vary. To avoid a monolithic, essentializing approach to incorporating HAI and HAB considerations with social work practice, we explore and identify relevant cultural components for a given client system within the context of assessment and intervention. In this chapter, we first provide a brief overview of the social work–related empirical literature on cultural differences in HAI. It is not our intent for this review to represent an exhaustive list, nor is it meant to serve as a basis for generalizations or definitive conclusions about groups of people who have companion animals. Rather, we seek to highlight areas identified through research that may be relevant for practice consideration. To help facilitate identification of both cultural and individual factors related to HAI within practice, we then offer specific areas for practice consideration adapted from a model of multiple influences on relationships with animals (Risley-Curtiss, Holley, & Wolf, 2006). For those interested in a broad, extensive examination of cross-cultural factors related to HAI, we suggest the book *Humans and Other Animals: Cross-Cultural Perspectives on Human–Animal Interactions*, authored by anthropologist Samantha Hurn and published in 2012.

Brief Overview of Research on Ethnic and Racial Differences Related to HAI and the HAB

Multicultural understandings of HAI can range widely and also may differ within subgroups of particular cultures and ethnic groups (Faver, 2013). Depending on the context, animals may hold roles as vastly different as food and work resources to therapeutic adjuncts and family members. Some cultural groups may see animals as especially suited for only some of these functions, whereas others still may prohibit certain roles (DeMello, 2012). Although some research has explored the varying cultural contexts of companion animals, there is not yet enough substantive data to draw generalizable conclusions about individuals within particular cultures (Brown, 2005; Risley-Curtiss, Holley, & Wolf, 2006).

To begin to address the dearth of research information on ethnic and cultural differences related to HAI, Risley-Curtiss, Holley, and Wolf (2006) conducted a random survey exploring relationships between the HAB and ethnic diversity in a large southwestern metropolitan area; a total of 587 interviews were completed. This exploratory study remains one of the only existing studies to explicitly consider variations in HAB experiences based on ethnic diversity. As summarized by Risley-Curtiss, Holley, and Wolf (2006), the most critical finding of this research was that across ethnic and racial groups, "the vast majority of dog and cat owners in this study said that their animal companions provide them with emotional support, unconditional love, and companionship and that they consider their animals to be family members" (p. 267). The ability to have meaningful bonds with animals transcended racial and ethnic differences.

Other findings from the study conducted by Risley-Curtiss, Holley, and Wolf (2006) revealed ethnic differences across three dimensions: companion animal ownership, care of companion animals, and relationships and beliefs related to companion animals. Concerning companion animal ownership, individuals who identified as American Indian were most likely to have companion animals (73.5 percent), followed by white people (65 percent), people of Hispanic or Spanish heritage (56.9 percent), African Americans (40.9 percent), Pacific Islanders (40 percent), and Asian Americans (37.5 percent) (Risley-Curtiss, Holley, & Wolf, 2006). With regard to animal care differences, individuals who identified as being of Hispanic or Spanish origin were less likely to have their animal spayed or neutered and were less likely to have a veterinarian; individuals who identified as white were more likely to have animals spayed or neutered at a young age (Risley-Curtiss, Holley, & Wolf, 2006). Individuals identifying as Hispanic or Spanish in origin were more likely to derive a sense of personal safety from their pet than were individuals identifying as members of the other groups, and individuals who identified as being of Asian descent were more likely to indicate they believed that animals do not feel pain (Risley-Curtiss, Holley, & Wolf, 2006).

Findings from existing research suggest that Asian cultural groups exhibit widely ranging attitudes toward dogs. Although in some cultures, particular species of animals are distinctly designated as either pets or food, Podberscek (2009) detailed a duality in a number of Asian cultures, where currently cats and dogs are considered "good to pet and eat." As cited in Sheade and Chandler (2012), research by Yeh (2008) suggested Japanese and Taiwanese populations have most heavily favored dogs and cats (over other varieties of companion animal) in roles assisting those experiencing schizophrenia and autism, whereas research by Iwahashi, Waga, and Ohta (2007) suggested that within Korean culture, dogs are viewed predominantly as food and considered unfit for the professional helping context. Findings in a study by Miura, Bradshaw, and Tanida (2002) indicated that among study participants, Japanese students were less than half as likely (41 percent) as British students (98 percent) to be accepting of assistance dogs in places where food was sold.

As summarized by Faver and Cavazos (2008), findings from research on Latino populations and companion animals are suggestive of the following:

That dogs are favored as companion animals, that many Latinos regard their companion animals as family members, and that a sense of safety is an important benefit for many guardians, in addition to companionship, emotional support, and unconditional love. It is likely that attitudes and practices regarding companion animals are affected by education and level of acculturation. (p. 258)

In additional research conducted by Faver and Cavazos (2008), Latino participants in their sample reported a rate of companion animal ownership (69.2 percent) that was comparable to the rate among all families in the United States (68.9 percent). Over half of the participants in their study reported companionship for children as a benefit of having a pet, and over two-fifths reported helping to teach children responsibility as an additional benefit (Faver & Cavazos, 2008).

Very little research literature focusing on the HAB in Middle Eastern cultures exists. Traditionally, some fear and distrust of dogs is noted by people from the Middle East, which stems from the wild and free-roaming dogs common in many Middle Eastern communities. Parish-Plass (2008) demonstrated, however, that AAT was effective in improving outcomes in a sample of Israeli children with attachment issues, and findings from a study of 52 Israeli households indicated that animals—including dogs— were viewed as family members (Shir-Vertesh, 2012).

African Americans have been particularly underrepresented in research on HAI and the HAB. In a survey of veterinary students, Brown (2002) found that white students were more likely to have animals, to have larger numbers of animals, and to sleep with those animals as compared with their African American peers; the white students also had higher scores on a standardized pet attachment scale. However, in later research, Brown (2005) cautioned that existing instruments of pet attachment may not be culturally sensitive enough: "The relationships between African Americans and animals may include feelings, beliefs or expressions of attachment not measurable by any [current] standard scale" (p. 117).

The multitude of religious faiths a person of any given cultural group may choose to practice is also a relevant factor that social workers need to be mindful of in considering HAI within a given client system. With regard to HAI and the HAB, the intermingling influences of specific cultures, ethnicities, spiritual backgrounds, and other aspects of diversity on particular client systems cannot be reduced to a static checklist of attributes for particular demographic groups. Rather, such influences must be assessed for and responded to as constellations of dynamic and interactive components that affect HAI experiences of clients.

HAI and Other Marginalized Groups

Beyond specific, traditional cultural groups, other forms of subcultures are created by sociocultural norms that marginalize individuals. Such distinctions may be transient or be present throughout the lifespan. Among these groups lie complex factors that can significantly affect how HAIs are experienced. Understanding the overall context that a culture creates also provides insight into how individuals may react to stressful animal-related events, but subdividing factors such as age, disability, and sexual or gender orientation (among others) make a nuanced understanding of the individual even more essential.

Older adults in the United States are one group for whom research and interventions have a legacy stretching back several more decades than most groups enjoy. Bikales's (1975) portrayal of an elderly woman's vital relationship with her dog, Lacey, demonstrated the mediating effect of pet attachment for older adults and was among the first to document this (Krause-Parello, 2008). Colombo et al. (2006) conducted a study that demonstrated that the simple inclusion of a companion animal in the lives of institutionalized, cognitively unimpaired elderly people increased their likelihood of socializing with others. Studies like these parallel many of the milieu-based interventions that also demonstrate physical benefits. The presence of animals provides engagement for those diagnosed with Alzheimer's disease at all stages of the disease's severity, as well as stress relief for caregivers. Beyond engaging and comforting, the presence of an animal may provide diagnostic clues for clinicians—for example, making concrete preparations for the care of companion animals is a highly predictive indicator of a suicide attempt for older adults (Lynch, Loane, Hally, & Wrigley, 2010).

Lesbian, gay, bisexual, transgender, and questioning (LGBTQ) individuals represent another group for whom significant factors related to companion animals are just beginning to emerge in the literature. Putney (2014) drew attention to the need for more research in this regard, as LGBTQ individuals (despite making significant strides toward greater recognition and inclusivity in recent years) still belong to a subgroup of people who experience disproportionate levels of psychological distress as a result of societal oppressions. In a qualitative study of older lesbian adults, Putney (2014) identified aspects of having a companion animal—specifically, love and caregiving—that had particular impact on four different areas of psychological well-being.

Among individuals living with stigmatized chronic health conditions, such as HIV and mental health disorders, HAI can have a positive effect. HAIs have been implemented in inpatient settings since the mid-1990s (Horowitz, 2010). A qualitative study by Wisdom, Saedi, and Green (2009) measured the supportive effect companion animals had in helping those with severe mental illness during their recovery. Wisdom et al. identified four themes that accord highly with the literature describing human–animal relationships in less specific groups: empathy and therapy, connections, pets as family, and self-efficacy and self-worth. In a sample of individuals with HIV, V. E. Hutton (2014) found that individuals with companion animals reported greater levels of well-being, as compared with individuals who did not have companion animals. V. E. Hutton suggested that the relationship with the companion animal might provide a buffer against associated stressful life experiences. In a sample of women living with HIV who had companion animals, participants reported that the animals provided a source of unconditional support, as well as a sense of purpose (Kabel, Khosla, & Teti, 2015).

Among a sample of youths who were homeless, a number of youths reported that their sole source of unconditional love was companion animals (Rew, 2000). Similarly, earlier research by R. S. Singer, Hart, and Zasloff (1995) found that over 96 percent of individuals who were acutely homeless declined housing if it meant leaving their animals. Guiding individuals who are homeless and have companion animals to resources that respect those relationships may be difficult, but it can be highly effective in establishing rapport.

Human relationships with animals may affect various aspects of a person's health (physical, mental, emotional, and social) across the lifespan; how these aspects then play out can vary significantly across cultural and other differences (Horowitz, 2008). Recognition of this and similar culturally relevant factors (such as differences in which types of animals a cultural group tends toward or away from) can enable social workers to respond in culturally sensitive ways to strengths or problems related to HAIs.

Assessing and Responding to Intersections of Multiple Sociocultural Influences on Relationships with Animals

Using data from qualitative interviews with women of color about their experiences with companion animals, Risley-Curtiss, Holley, Cruickshank, et al. (2006) developed a model of the multiple interactive influences of these women's relationships with their animals. Although developed from interview data with women of particular ethnic backgrounds, the aspects identified within this model can be extrapolated to other ethnic groups and genders. Moreover, historically, many conceptual models have been white- and male-centric; with an eye toward decentering such models, we suggest using Risley-Curtiss et al.'s model as a framework to help identify and inform cultural considerations related to HAI and social work practice and henceforth refer to it as the multiple influences on relationships with animals model (MIRA).

The MIRA, as conceptualized by Risley-Curtiss, Holley, Cruickshank, et al. (2006, p. 443), outlines the following four spheres of influence on relationships with animals for practice consideration, with each sphere embedded within and interactive with the broader subsequent spheres:

1. Individual sphere: individual's perceptions and experiences
   - Opportunities to interact with animals (for example, strays, family pets, work animals)
   - Initial feelings of attachment to animals (for example, a sense of connection)
   - Perceptions of what animals and humans bring to the relationship (for example, comfort, protection)
   - Perceptions of the views of family and social groups about human–animal relationships (for example, whether the animal is a family member or companion)

- Personal experiences that may draw one to seek relationships with animals (for example, no human confidantes)

2. Family sphere—family's perceptions and experiences
   - Same as individual views and experiences

3. Intersections of social identity sphere—perceptions and experiences of peers at intersections of ethnicity; national origin; social class; and the urban, suburban, or rural setting in which the family or individual resides
   - Same as individual and family experiences
   - Housing type
   - Resources available to care for animals
   - Beliefs about animals related to intersections of groups

4. Dominant culture perceptions sphere—perceptions of the dominant, power-holding, or historically privileged group within a given society or culture
   - Views of appropriate purposes and positions of various animals for companionship, work, protection, and food
   - Beliefs about how various animals are to be treated as depicted in laws, media, people's daily care of animals, and economic practices

This model assumes that there are competing views about animals within each sphere and the views about and relationships with animals may change over time (Risley-Curtiss, Holley, Cruickshank, et al., 2006). These spheres offer starting points for culturally responsive inclusion of HAI considerations within social work practice; such multilevel spheres also suggest that there are likely multilevel—micro, mezzo, and macro—social work interventions that may be relevant with regard to HAI within given cultural contexts (Risley-Curtiss, Holley, Cruickshank, et al., 2006). In working with clients, social workers can draw from these spheres to help formulate questions that invite clients to share their unique perspectives on the importance and impact of HAI in their daily lives.

8

Companion Animal Loss

Much of the initial proposal for this book was drafted in the ward of an animal hospital. One of the authors, Janet, wrote on her cell phone using a Word app while cradling her gravely ill 16-year-old dog, Jazzie, who had been hospitalized for diagnostics and supportive care. Janet had found Jazzie 15 years earlier in the middle of a busy intersection while driving to her case management job at a community mental health center. She stopped her car in the middle of the intersection and opened the door, and in jumped the little black-and-white dog. After having no success in finding who he belonged to, she adopted him and named him Jazz (which quickly became Jazzie) because he reminded her of jazz music when he pranced. Jazzie became the most constant companion of Janet's adult life; he was at her side through two additional degree programs, numerous jobs, homes, relationships, marriage, divorce, life-threatening illness, travels, and the simple experiences of everyday life. Jazzie had lost his hearing a couple of years before the hospitalization and had other aging issues, but he was in reasonably good health until he developed unexplained severe weakness and fatigue. Initially, Janet laid half in, half out of Jazzie's cage so she could be alongside him while writing on her cell phone app. Later, a vet tech kindly gave Janet a chair to sit on and a large cushion for Jazzie to rest on Janet's lap, helped adjust Jazzie's IVs and move him to the cushion, and found an outlet to keep Janet's phone charged. Janet and Scott (the other author) communicated drafts and ideas through e-mails and texts, and three days of writing progressed thus, with Jazzie cradled in Janet's lap at the animal hospital ward.

Working on the proposal for this book was a helpful focal point, as Janet was consumed with an agonizing question faced by many who are struggling with the ailments of an elderly companion animal: Am I extending his life or prolonging his suffering? At the end of the week, after some improvement, Jazzie was discharged home with a care plan. He was home overnight, only to be brought back to the hospital the next day because of the severe worsening of his symptoms. After consulting with the vet and her family, Janet made the decision to euthanize Jazzie in a memorial garden in the yard outside the veterinary clinic—he loved the outdoors—surrounded by his family who loved him. They took his body home and buried him in the backyard in "his" hole (a hole he loved to dig in while Janet gardened). The death of Jazzie was a profound loss, and grieving that loss will be an ongoing, lifelong process for Janet.

Although many self-identified animal lovers can relate to Janet's experience of losing Jazzie, the loss of a companion animal can occur and be experienced in a myriad of different ways. As with humans, one can lose a companion animal to death. The death of a companion animal may be sudden and accidental, a slow deterioration due to natural causes, a planned occurrence through euthanasia, or the result of a brutal act of violence. Companion animal loss, however, is not limited to when a companion animal dies. A person may also have to surrender a companion animal if he or she is no longer able to care for that animal. Through placements in nursing homes and correction facilities and by serving military tours of duty, people may temporarily or permanently lose their companion animals. A child may be separated from a beloved companion animal through foster home placement or may have an adult caregiver get rid of his or her companion animal without the child's consent. Separation from one's companion animal may also occur forcibly through legal means when animals are removed from a person's care because of negligence or abuse; as with human abuse and neglect situations, the person who is abusing or neglecting the companion animal may nonetheless have an attachment to that animal. A companion animal may disappear (he or she may have been taken or gotten out of the house and become lost) and never be found again despite extensive searching. The process of losing a companion animal can distinctly differ from the loss of a human companion in numerous ways, such as when one has to give up an animal because the place one needs to move to—as a result of homelessness (Slatter, Lloyd, & King, 2012), health issues that require residence in a nursing home or inpatient services, natural disaster (Scott, 2008; Zottarelli, 2010), or domestic violence (Ascione, Weber, Thompson, Heath, Maruyama, & Hayashi, 2013)—does not permit companion animals on the premises; make a choice to euthanize one's companion animal (Dawson & Campbell, 2009); or otherwise face the invalidation and lack of societal recognition for grieving related to companion animal loss. Finally, a person may lose his or her companion animal because of his or her own death; companion animals are increasingly being identified as survivors in obituaries, which is indicative of their perceived family status in many households (Wilson et al., 2013).

Social workers working with individuals affected by companion animal loss must be aware of and responsive to dimensions of companion animal loss that are both similar to and different from the loss of humans so that they may effectively support their clients through what may be a very traumatic and difficult experience. In this chapter, we explore various aspects of companion animal loss experiences and delineate corresponding areas for social work assessment and intervention, including micro and macro dimensions of practice.

Starting Where the Client Is At: Understanding the Internal Effect of Companion Animal Loss

"With great love comes great grief" (Carmack, 2003, p. 5). Stroebe, Hansson, Schut, Stroebe, and Van den Blink (2008) distinguished between *grief*, which they defined as the internal experience of loss, and *mourning*, which they defined as the external behaviors and rituals—which are highly influenced by cultural context, norms, and spiritual beliefs—through which grief is expressed; the term *bereavement* is more broadly defined as experiencing loss as a result of a death. Janet experienced profound grief on Jazzie's death through euthanasia and actively mourned his loss; she loved Jazzie tremendously, had lived with him and considered him part of her family for 15 years, and had highly integrated her interactions with him into her daily life routines. The depth of grief a client may experience after the loss of a companion animal is related to each of the following factors: the perceived nature of the relationship (Packman et al., 2014), the strength of attachment (Lee & Surething, 2013; Packman, Field, Carmack, & Ronen, 2011; Planchon, Templer, Stokes, & Keller, 2002), the longevity of the relationship (Packman et al., 2011), the cause of death

(Lee & Surething, 2013; Planchon et al., 2002) in instances of loss due to death, and the resultant loss of daily interactions (Packman et al., 2014). Pomeroy and Garcia (2008) referred to such resultant losses as *secondary losses*; for instance, *primary loss* refers to the actual loss of Jazzie, whereas *secondary loss* refers to all of the things Janet lost as a result Jazzie's death, such as daily interactions, the role as his caregiver, the emotional comfort derived from him in times of stress, and so forth. Because each person is unique, each loss experience is also unique; to effectively respond to a client's needs related to the loss of a companion animal, a social worker needs to understand the combined impact of factors (noted above) on that individual's grief intensity and within his or her cultural and social contexts.

The perceived nature of a relationship between people and their respective companion animals varies widely. Although many people consider their companion animals to be family members (Toray, 2004), others ascribe low status to companion animals and consider them to be property that may be valuable but ultimately is expendable or replaceable (Hogan & Hoy, 2015). As noted in previous chapters but worth repeating, according to the 2015–2016 APPA Survey—the largest demographic survey of households with companion animals in the United States—65 percent of U.S. households reported having at least one companion animal, and the majority of these reported that they considered their companion animals to be family members. Gerwolls and Labott (1994) assessed whether the loss experienced on the death of a companion animal was different from loss experienced on the death of a human family member (parent, child, or spouse). They reported that at eight weeks and six months after the loss, the differences in grief scores between the two groups were not significant. Packman et al. (2011) found no statistically significant differences in mourning expressions between a sample of individuals who had lost companion animals to death and a sample of individuals who had lost spouses to death. Although both studies used convenience samples and cannot be generalized to all people who have companion animals because of the wide variance in how companion animals may be regarded, such findings do suggest that the loss experienced on the death of a companion animal truly perceived as an immediate family member can parallel the loss experienced on the death of human immediate family members. Although Janet viewed Jazzie as a beloved immediate family member and subsequently had a tremendous grief reaction, others who lose companion animals may have less regard for them and subsequently may experience minimal grief.

The notion of attachment, as discussed in previous chapters of this book, is increasingly used to explain and operationalize the strength of the emotional connection in the HAB literature (Rockett & Carr, 2014). To recap, attachment theory originated in the work of Bowlby (1969), who defined attachment as a "lasting connectedness" between specific individuals across time and space in which proximity is sought and an individual may function as a secure base. Rockett and Carr (2014), in their review of the literature on attachment theory and animals, found extensive use of conceptualizations of animals as attachment figures for humans, as well as variations in the quality of attachment toward animals. Increasingly, attachment theory has also been used to understand and explain the HAB. In August 2014, Kenneth Shapiro, board president of the Animals and Society Institute, along with Jill Howard Church, the institute's communications director, blogged,

> Human-Animal Studies is a field in search of a paradigm, a primary theoretical base. Attachment theory appears more and more to be a primary contender for this role. . . . [Attachment] theory is receiving considerable attention both empirically and conceptually. The theory involves the establishment of strong bonds in which other individuals function as a secure base or anchor and, in times of distress, as a safe haven. The thrust of the literature is that this bond can be formed across species.
>
> This has important policy implications, for it allows that humans can form strong bonds with nonhuman animals that may resemble those formed between humans. Beyond the common role of being in the dependent and subordinate position, a nonhuman animal can be a primary source of emotional comfort. (paras. 4–5)

In the example given at the beginning of this chapter, one may discern that Janet was and is very emotionally attached to Jazzie: He was a source of continuity, akin to a secure base, through the various changes and challenges she experienced in their 15 years together. The intensity of her internal grief experience corresponded with the level of attachment she had and has for Jazzie, whereas a person with minimal attachment to a companion animal who has died is likely to have a much less intense internal reaction. The strength of attachment to a companion animal may deepen over time; Packman et al. (2011) found that, along with strength of attachment, the longevity of a relationship with a companion animal was a significant predictor of increased grief intensity. The level of attachment and the longevity of that human–companion animal relationship are hence important aspects of understanding the impact of a companion animal loss on a particular individual. The time in one's life in which one obtained the animal may also have significance and meaning related to attachment; for instance, Janet found Jazzie shortly after moving out to live on her own as a young adult, and he was her first dog.

Assessment of companion animal attachment and related factors can take place through a variety of means. Standardized instruments are available for this purpose and include the Lexington Attachment to Pets Scale (Johnson, Garrity, & Stallones, 1992); however, merely asking an open-ended question such as "Can you tell me about [insert name of animal]?" can generate dialogue about the perceived nature of the relationship and level of attachment. Prefacing such an open-ended question by explicitly validating the possibility of strong attachment and an equally strong grief reaction may be crucial in enabling a person to feel comfortable expressing his or her feelings, especially when such feelings are contrary to dominant cultural norms and beliefs related to companion animal loss. As put by Packman et al. (2014),

> The clinical setting needs to be an environment in which clients are invited to express not only the depth of loss but also the nature of the relationship. Often the bereaved are tentative when they are not sure of others' recognition of their relationships with their companion animals. They are hesitant to say, "she was my baby" or "she was my best friend, my soul mate." But when the clinician invites such disclosure by affirming "frequently people may describe their pets as their baby, their child, a member of their family and that this is the hardest loss they have ever experienced," people are more likely to acknowledge such feelings. They can hold onto the possibility that the clinician will be accepting and validating of both the intensity of their feelings and the

nature of their relationship and not feel the embarrassment, and even shame, they may have in other settings. (p. 350)

As with all areas of social work practice, self-awareness is of ongoing importance; transference and projection of one's own reactions must be monitored. Although a social worker may ascribe family status and intrinsic value to companion animals, that social worker must not project beliefs onto clients. A client who is minimally attached to his or her companion animal may experience little or no subsequent grief over the loss of that animal and may not have any need for additional exploration of or support for the loss experience.

Assessment of possible secondary losses related to the loss of a companion animal is also important in supporting a client affected by the loss of a companion animal. For 15 years, Jazzie lived in Janet's home, slept beside her, was her daily companion, and shared many daily routines with her; each of these was a secondary loss. In addition to these immediate secondary losses, other secondary losses were experienced over time. For example, Jazzie died in the fall; having spent many springs gardening with Jazzie romping and digging alongside of her, Janet experienced the loss of her "co-gardener's" company in the year that followed. To understand the extent to which the secondary losses of a companion animal may disrupt a client's daily life, it is important to assess (a) how long a client has had a particular companion animal, (b) how that animal fits in with the client's daily life or routine, (c) what role or roles the companion animal may occupy (for example, friend, family member, surrogate child, protector) in the life of the client, and (d) what roles the client holds in relation to the animal (for example, caregiver, guardian). Asking questions about these areas enables an individual to share the extent to which the loss of a companion animal may disrupt his or her daily life routine and functioning. Such questions can also identify areas where supports and coping strategies may be helpful in dealing with the impact of the loss.

A companion animal's death can occur in a variety of ways. The cause of death may be natural causes, sudden and accidental, an intentional act of violence or abuse, or a planned euthanasia. Most companion animals have shorter lifespans than humans do, so an individual with a companion animal is likely to outlive the companion animal. As cats, dogs, and other typical companion animal species age, they experience a gradual decline in physical and cognitive functioning, much as aging humans do. An elderly companion animal may have increasingly limited mobility, senses, bowel and bladder control, and organ functioning, any of which may cause emotional stress or entail additional caregiving responsibilities for the person the animal belongs to. The animal may eventually die of natural causes, or because of painful, progressive, or incurable illness, a person may opt to euthanize his or her animal. Choosing euthanasia may result in feelings of guilt over the death of one's companion animal; when euthanasia is chosen at least partly because one cannot afford treatment, guilt can be further exacerbated (Dawson & Campbell, 2009). Ambivalence regarding euthanasia can be further complicated "by the fact that animals cannot communicate their physical or emotional states verbally to people" (Dawson & Campbell, 2009, p. 104). One cannot ask one's companion animal what that animal's wishes are regarding euthanasia; instead, one must decide what to do on the basis of the animal's prognosis, veterinary recommendations, available resources, and other factors.

Watching one's companion animal decline and lose quality of life and contemplating euthanasia can evoke what is referred to "anticipatory grief." Stroebe et al. (2008) explained *anticipatory grief* as any grief reaction felt in response to an impending loss. Validation of a client's feelings and concerns and collaboration with veterinary professionals can support clients facing difficult end-of-life scenarios with their companion animals. With regard to collaborating with veterinary staff, a person may need support in a variety of ways: access to veterinary services; linkage to or advocacy for clear information about the animal's diagnosis, the prognosis, and pros and cons of available treatment options; linkage to financial resources that may help cover the cost of treatments; and provision of behavioral change benchmarks that can assist with quality-of-life determinations (Hogan & Hoy, 2015).

Many people choose to remain with their companion animals during the actual euthanasia. Explicit education about the euthanasia process may help prepare a person or family to witness it; for instance, an animal may have involuntary spasms and movements, appear to continue breathing, or have other reactions that can be extremely distressing to witness if one is not aware of the possibility beforehand. The euthanasia may or may not be experienced as a traumatic event, and screening and support for trauma symptoms and suicidal ideation may be necessary (Packman et al., 2014).

The unexpected accidental death of one's companion animal—such as when a pet is struck by a car—can also potentially be experienced as a traumatic event. Moreover, such an incident may elicit an intense loss and grief experience because the animal has died prematurely and possibly in a preventable manner. Guilt and regret regarding whether or how the death may have been prevented can be a significant source of distress for those who have lost companion animals in such a way. Accidental companion animal death was highly correlated with an extended grief process (Planchon et al., 2002). As when a beloved companion animal is euthanized, trauma and suicidal ideation should be assessed for and addressed in the human client as needed.

Companion animals also die as a result of acts of intentional violence, as noted in chapter 6 of this book. Such violent and intentional companion animal deaths may occur through extensions of abuse in family violence situations (Hardesty, Khaw, Ridgway, Weber, & Miles, 2013), as a result of cruel "pranks" by those with low regard for the intrinsic value of other species, or at the hands of those with antisocial traits who enjoy inflicting suffering on vulnerable beings. In a statewide sample of children with companion animals who lived in households with IPV, McDonald et al. (2014) found that witnessing intentional violence toward or killing of one's companion animal was the strongest predictor of future clinical levels of anxiety and depression. In qualitative research with a subgroup of this sample of children, McDonald et al. (2014) also found that children attempted to intervene and protect their companion animals and were willing to put themselves in harm's way to do so.

Because animals have the status of property in the United States, the legal consequences for violently killing an animal are nominal compared with the legal consequences of violently killing a human. A person may sue for compensation related to emotional pain and suffering or for the monetary value of the animal in civil court, and the perpetrator of the animal's death may be charged with and convicted of animal cruelty, which may be a misdemeanor or a felony depending on the state in which the crime was committed. For a person who considered the animal that was killed to be a beloved and an immediate family member, such consequence disparities can be difficult to reconcile and can further exacerbate the intensity of his or her grief. In such situations, it is imperative that trauma symptoms, suicidal and homicidal ideations, and anxiety and depression should be assessed for and responded to; further, support and advocacy in any resulting legal processes should be provided. In short, when an individual who considers his or her companion animal to be a beloved family member loses that animal to death as a result of another's deliberate violence, the supports offered should parallel those offered— to the extent possible—when an individual experiences the death of a human companion due to violence.

Recognizing and Responding to Nondeath Types of Companion Animal Loss

The loss of a companion animal is not limited to scenarios in which the animal dies. An individual may experience companion animal loss and the impact of that loss in a variety of ways (depending on factors discussed in the previous section). Recognizing, validating, and responding to these other types of companion animal loss are crucial in supporting a client experiencing grief related to that loss. A person may choose to surrender a beloved companion animal to a shelter; this loss may be a decision related to being unable to afford or otherwise provide for the animal's needs and can result in tremendous grief and guilt. In an exploratory study with individuals who had given up companion animals because of homelessness, Slatter et al. (2012) found the impact of giving up the companion animal to be significant. Sadly, one has only to spend a day in the intake area of a busy humane society to witness such scenarios. To prevent these types of surrenders, what are referred to as "human–animal support services" are increasingly being offered through organizations such as PAWS (Gorczyca et al., 2010; Pets Are Wonderful Support, n.d.-a) and through targeted program development at humane societies and other animal welfare organizations. The mission of PAWS, a nonprofit located in California, is "to preserve, support and nurture the human-animal bond for those most vulnerable in our community" (PAWS, n.d.-a, PAWS Mission section, para. 1). The PAWS (n.d.-b) Web site describes numerous direct services and supports targeted at accomplishing their mission:

- PET FOOD BANK: On-site and home delivery of pet food and supplies
- VETERINARY SERVICES: Financial assistance for preventative, comprehensive and emergency veterinary care provided by our veterinary volunteers and partners
- IN-HOME cat care, dog walking, transportation and emergency foster care
- GROOMING (paras. 3–7)

PAWS also offers information and referrals for housing, licensing, microchips, and other needed resources.

In addition to providing linkage and referrals to such direct service supports, social workers can also work at the macro level to develop programming for human–animal support services where none currently exist. PAWS created a start-up kit for communities that wish to develop such programming (PAWS, 2009). Social workers can also reach out to local humane societies to develop partnerships that provide human–animal support services. For instance, through collaboration with the University of Toledo Social Work Program and other community entities, the TAHS has developed programming to meet a number of common needs and offers temporary foster care in emergency situations (eviction or homelessness, domestic violence, hospitalization, and so forth); a behavior help line to address behavior-related surrenders; mobile pet food and litter delivery; and information and referrals to pet-friendly housing and low-cost or free spay, neuter, and vaccination services. To facilitate support of the HAB and related programming, in partnership with the University of Toledo, the TAHS has also developed an advanced MSW internship placement. Humane Ohio, a nonprofit and the primary provider of low- or no-cost spaying, neutering, and vaccination services in the Toledo area, works closely with the TAHS and provides a free pet food bank. In deployment situations, organizations such as Guardian Angels for Soldiers' Pets have incorporated and are offering long-term fostering; information is available on their Web site: http://guardianangelsforsoldierspet.org/. Because of social workers' required training and professional mission, social workers are uniquely situated not only to provide direct service linkage and grief support but also to facilitate community organizing and program development related to such human–animal support services.

Social workers also have training in social policy formulation and processes, which can be used to help institutionalize human–animal supports at state and federal levels. As a result of mass outrage, advocacy, and activism, a U.S. federal law referred to as Pet Evacuation and Transportation Standards (better known as the PETS Act) was passed in August 2006; this law requires local and state governments to include companion animals in evacuation planning and provides federal money for pet-friendly shelters (Scott, 2008). Before Hurricane Katrina, people being evacuated because of disasters in the United States could not bring their companion animals to shelters, and no alternative accommodations for the companion animals were provided. People needing to use shelters during disasters or mass evacuations—primarily people who did not have the means of affording pet-friendly hotels or other alternatives—were forced to choose between refusing to evacuate to remain with companion animals or evacuating and abandoning their companion animals (Zottarelli, 2010). During Hurricane Katrina, companion animal loss received extensive media exposure:

> When the devastating tragedy of Hurricane Katrina struck New Orleans in August 2005, the whole world watched as countless indelible images and stories were broadcast on our television and computer screens. Among them were the unforgettable faces of the thousands of animals left stranded by the terrible storm and all too fragile levees. (Scott, 2008, p. vii)

As with many social injustice situations, the situation was crystallized through a single image and story:

> Among the thousands of crushing moments from last week's deadly hurricane, one image brought the anguish home to many: a tearful little boy torn from his dog while being shuttled to safety.
>
> It tugged at the heartstrings, prompting an outpouring from around the country of people on the hunt for both the boy and his dog Snowball in hopes of a reunion. . . .
>
> The boy was among the thousands sheltered at the Super-dome after the hurricane. But when he went to board a bus to

be evacuated to Houston, a police officer took the dog away. The boy cried out—"Snowball! Snowball!"—then vomited in distress.

The confrontation was first reported by The Associated Press. Authorities say they don't know where the boy or his family ended up. ("Searchers Try to Reunite Boy, Dog," 2005)

To our knowledge, the boy and Snowball were never reunited, and the fate of Snowball remains unknown.

Although there is now institutionalized support at the federal, state, and local levels for human–animal support services during mass disasters, there are numerous other scenarios in which companion animal loss occurs involuntarily for which human–animal supports are not widely available. A person may be separated from his or her companion animal involuntarily as a result of incarceration, placement in foster care, or placement in a nursing home facility. In each instance, the separation may be temporary or permanent, depending on the social supports and resources available. Advocating for and arranging visits with companion animals may be feasible for children in foster care or adults in nursing homes, and it should be sought whenever possible and desired by clients. A social worker can also assist a person facing incarceration with planning for his or her companion animal's well-being; even if the separation is anticipated to be long term or permanent, the knowledge that the companion animal will be cared for may relieve some distress.

Finally, a person may face companion animal loss because of that person's own impending death. Formally arranging for the well-being of one's animal after one's death is increasingly done through inclusion of companion animals in wills or through fee-based programs offered by humane societies that provide guaranteed care and placement for companion animals after the death of the purchaser or designee. Provisions to care for a companion animal after a person's death can also be arranged through a person's informal social support system. In particular, social workers in hospice, hospitals, and other end-of-life settings should assess for these needs and support these provisions as needed; knowing that a surviving companion animal will be taken care of can provide a dying person with much-needed closure and peace at the end of his or her life.

Mourning, Disenfranchised Grief, and Continuing Bonds

People across cultures and throughout a substantive amount of human history have formed attachments to members of other species, enjoyed their companionship, and grieved their loss (Hurn, 2012). In contrast, an individual's external expressions of such grief, also known as mourning, as well as the response of the individual's community to his or her expressed grief and mourning, are diverse and culturally mediated (Stroebe et al., 2008). Normative expectations of rituals (funerals, memorials, and the like) and comfort-focused customs (for example, family gatherings, bringing food to the bereaved)—varying by culture, spiritual tradition, and other factors—are in place in contemporary U.S. society to facilitate community support and recognition of the loss of a human. In contrast, such widespread recognition and normative expectations of communal support are absent for one experiencing the loss of a companion animal; such a loss is often not recognized as a legitimate cause for intense grief and subsequent mourning. These unrecognized losses are described by Doka (2008) as "disenfranchised grief."

> Disenfranchised grief, by its very nature, precludes social support. . . . Empathic failure frequently occurs within the social support systems of those grieving the death of a pet. Empathic failure, or "the failure of one part of a system to understand the meaning of another" (Neimeyer & Jordan, 2002, p. 96), exists in which people do not understand the depth of the human-pet relationship. Their social system fails to understand the meaning and experience of their relationship, which is typically based on unconditional love, continuing presence, support, and consistent companionship. (Packman et al., 2014, pp. 334–335)

Even well-intentioned people may inadvertently invalidate the unique relationship and bond that may exist between a person and his or her deceased companion animal through comments such as "it's just a cat" and "you can always get another one." In contrast, "it would be considered inappropriate to tell a new widower to find a new wife" (Packman et al., 2011, p. 343). Participants in study conducted by Packman et al. (2014) expressed intensive grief experiences, for example, "the loss of Merlin has been the hardest experience of my life" (p. 346) and "I'm in such pain that I can hardly function" (p. 346). These same participants described environments in which their grief was disenfranchised:

> One of the hardest parts is now when you feel so alone because there are no gathering of friends and relatives, no published obituary, no one bringing food, etc. It is as if no one knows how real and deep the loss of unconditional love can be and you feel you need to hide or you cannot be true to yourself. (Packman et al., 2014, p. 343)

In working with a client who is dealing with companion animal loss, it is crucial that the social worker validate the experienced impact of the client's companion animal loss while actively supporting the client in navigating invalidating environments. To do so, the social worker should assess the client's needs and then meet those needs by linking the client to validating peer support through pet loss groups (face-to-face or online), providing or referring the client to grief counseling, and supporting or facilitating client expressions of existential or spiritual meanings and mourning behaviors. At the macro practice level, social workers also need to develop an awareness of and advocate for changes in factors that perpetuate client experiences of disenfranchised grief. For instance, most workplace policies do not offer bereavement leave for companion animal loss (Doka, 2008), forcing a bereaved person to use vacation or sick time if time away from work is needed as a result of the loss.

The *continuing bonds framework*, which conceptualizes death as loss that is permanent at the physical level but does not preclude maintaining an ongoing bond with the one who has died (Field, Nichols, Holen, & Horowitz, 1999), has been introduced into companion animal loss literature (Packman et al., 2011). In an exploratory study, Packman, Carmack, and Ronen (2011–2012) identified the following continuing bonds expressions as present to varying degrees among participants and called for clinicians to explore such expressions as sources of comfort or distress:

- sensing the presence and continuing connection with their deceased pet
- thinking that they heard or felt their pet's sounds or movements (i.e., intrusive symptoms)

- talking to their deceased pet
- recalling fond memories
- dreaming of the pet
- holding on to or using special belongings of their pet in order to feel close
- creating memorials, shrines, or attending special events [for example, creating rituals] in tribute to their deceased pet
- being drawn to places associated with their deceased pet
- learning lessons from their pet
- being influenced by the pet in making everyday decisions and choices
- attempting to carry out or live up to the deceased pet's wishes
- having thoughts of being reunited with the pet (p. 339)

In this study, they found that the majority participants exhibited and derived comfort from recalling fond memories, using rituals, and recognizing the animal's presence in dreams. Packman et al. (2011–2012) concluded that offering clients opportunities to explore their experiences related to continuing bonds expressions constituted an actively supportive clinician response:

> Frequently, people are hesitant to share their experiences of CB [continuing bonds] for fear that they will be perceived as "crazy" or "going off the deep end" . . . yet when given the invitation to talk about their experience in a supportive validating setting, often they are willing, and grateful, for the opportunity to describe and discuss their experiences. In the sharing of these experiences, some are looking for validation that these experiences are not "weird" or "crazy." On the other hand, others are not necessarily seeking validation but instead a safe place in which to tell their stories and describe their experiences. (p. 349)

Religious, spiritual, and existential beliefs related to companion animal death are potentially salient, culturally mediated aspects of how grief related to companion animal loss is experienced (Faver, 2009; Hanrahan, 2011; Lee & Surething, 2013). Within the Packman et al. (2014) study of continuing bonds expressions among those who lost companion animals to death, spiritual beliefs related to whether participants would be reunited with their animals were salient. Sixty-four percent of participants believed that they would be reunited with their companion animals in some fashion and found comfort in this. Other participants were not sure of being reunited because of religious teachings, whereas still others indicated they believed they would never be reunited because of religious teachings: For one participant, "because she had been taught by her church that pets do not go to Heaven, for her the finality of never seeing her animal again was exacerbating her grief experience and resulting in excruciating grief" (Packman et al., 2014, p. 352). It is important to explicitly ask about such spiritual, existential, and religious beliefs and to assist with linkages to validating pastoral care or other appropriate resources as needed or desired by the client.

Conclusion

Both increased recognition of and more empathic responses to client experiences of companion animal loss are needed within social work practice. Although not all clients will be adversely affected by the loss of a companion animal, many individuals consider companion animals to be members of their families and experience substantial grief. Clients' grief experiences may be compounded by social contexts in which their grief is disenfranchised. In addition to direct services and micro practice social responses, there is also a need to address the disenfranchisement of companion animal loss at the macro practice level. Through continued development of human–animal support services and advocacy for policies that recognize and legitimize companion animal loss, the factors that systematically create empathic failure in clients' environments can begin to be ameliorated.

9

Understanding the Therapeutic Roles of Animals

The benefits of HAI can occur along physical, psychological, emotional, and social dimensions. Certainly not everyone may experience them; as explored in chapter 7, cultural and other personal considerations are imperative in determining whether HAI may be acceptable or therapeutic. A person who has not had many experiences with animals may not be comfortable with HAI, and some people may indicate apathy toward or a dislike of animals. People with severe allergies, people who fear animals, and people who have a history of animal abuse may also not find HAI beneficial and may not be appropriate candidates for animal-assisted supports. As with other aspects of social work practice, we need to start where the client is at. Given that the majority of U.S. households report having companion animals, as mentioned in previous chapters, it is highly likely that social workers will encounter clients who will benefit from HAI. Such benefits may be particularly effective for people with stressors or disabilities that may be ameliorated through interactions with animals. In such instances, interactions with animals can be specifically therapeutic; therapeutic roles of animals can entail anything from minimal to extensive training to convey HAI benefits. Although human benefits derived through HAI continue to emerge in research literature, the labels used to refer to the involved animals are inconsistent, resulting in confusion among health care professionals, researchers, policymakers, individuals with disabilities, and regulatory agencies (Parenti, Foreman, Meade, & Wirth, 2013). In a literature review, Mills and Yeager (2012) found 12 definitions describing types of therapeutic animals in health care and social services contexts. In an extensive review of literature related to definitions of therapeutic roles of animals, Parenti et al. (2013)

concluded that the therapeutic roles and functions of animals providing HAI benefits to individuals can be differentiated by five factors: the nature of the disability- or impairment-related assistance and alleviation provided by the animal, the level of training required by the animal to provide the assistance or support, the attributes of the animal's human handler, the existence of certifications or standards to help guide the training or involvement of the animal, and the extent of the legal protections enabling the handler to have public access with the animal. In this chapter, we review and apply these dimensions to delineate the basic therapeutic roles of animals on a continuum ranging from animals with the least training to animals with the most training. These roles are as follows: emotional support animals, visitation animals, therapy animals, and assistance or service animals. We also discuss ethical considerations related to animals in these therapeutic roles.

Differentiating the Therapeutic Roles of Animals

The Nature of Assistance Provided by the Animal

Through an extensive review of literature, Parenti et al. (2013) identified five specific factors crucial in understanding the nature of the therapeutic role of the animal in HAI. The nature of the assistance provided by the animal, one of the factors explicated by Parenti et al. (2013), falls into two categories: (1) naturalistic or passive assistance and (2) task-trained or active assistance. *Naturalistic* or *passive assistance* refers to HAI benefits that are conveyed through the presence of and everyday, natural interactions with an animal. Simply by interacting with the animal and being in its presence, a person may experience symptom reduction or improved quality of life through the physical, psychological, social, and emotional benefits (as detailed in chapter 3) that occur through HAI. Although not technically passive, such assistance can be termed such, as the animal is not actively performing specific tasks for the explicit purpose of providing assistance to a person. An example of this would be a person who alleviates feelings of anxiety by holding and stroking a cat; through this action, a person may literally feel better and experience a decrease in anxiety through the oxytocin release, slowed respiration, and cortisol and adrenaline decreases associated with physical HAI. The cat is not doing anything in particular other than being receptive to the stroking action. In contrast, *task-trained assistance* refers to an animal actively completing activities or tasks that are directly targeted at reducing specific symptoms or impairment related to a person's disability. Parenti et al. (2013) offered the following examples of task-trained or active assistance: retrieving items to reduce impairment related to physical disability, alerting to sounds to reduce impairment related to hearing disability, disrupting trauma-related flashbacks to reduce impairment related to psychological disability, and guiding to a specific location to reduce impairment related to visual disability.

Necessary Training

The level of training needed by the animal to provide therapeutic assistance or support ranges widely, from basic socialization to intensive task completion–focused training, typically referred to as *assistance* or *service dog training* (Parenti et al., 2013). To provide naturalistic or passive support and thereby convey the HAI benefits associated with such support, an animal needs to be able to interact safely and comfortably with at least some humans. Hence, they need basic socialization; informal training on housebreaking and other basic acceptable, desirable, and expected behaviors in a given household or context; and a disposition that is generally nonaggressive and friendly. This essentially describes what is needed for an animal to be a companion animal or pet (or an emotional support animal [ESA], as described later in this chapter). In contrast, an animal who will be going into public settings, such as hospitals, nursing homes, or schools, and interacting with unknown people on a regular basis needs additional training beyond what is needed for a companion animal (or an ESA). Typically, such animals are dogs who have completed obedience training to pass a therapy dog evaluation conducted by one of several national therapy dog groups (further discussed in the Therapy Dogs section of this chapter). These evaluations may require the dog to be able to complete tasks such as walking calmly on a loose lead (heeling); sitting and staying in place; interacting with and being brushed by an unknown person; and not reacting to wheelchairs, walkers, strange dogs, and crowds, along with other tasks associated with providing naturalistic assistance in public places. Animals who provide task-related or active assistance, in addition to being able to perform basic obedience commands and other behaviors associated with safety in public settings, also must be able to complete specific tasks related to a particular disability, typically in a much wider range of public settings, such as restaurants, grocery stores, and the like. To acquire these skills, animals who provide task-related or active assistance need extensive training.

Attributes of the Animal's Primary Human Handler

As explained by Parenti et al. (2013), the person who is handling the animal may be performing one of three roles: The person may be the recipient of the HAI benefits, that is, the primary beneficiary of the HAI benefits that are being conveyed by the animal; the person may be a volunteer who is seeking to promote HAI benefits for an individual or group; or the person may be a health care professional (such as a social worker) who is working with an animal and a client to convey HAI benefits as an adjunct to other treatment benefits within the scope of professional service provision. The person who is both the primary beneficiary of HAI benefits and the primary handler of an animal in a therapeutic role is typically either a person with a disability who has a task-trained service dog or a person with a disability who lives with a companion animal and receives naturalistic or passive benefits through the animal's presence (this animal may be legally recognized as an ESA, as described in the ESAs section of this chapter). A volunteer handler is someone who brings an animal (typically an animal who has passed a therapy dog evaluation) to visit with and provide HAI benefits to a particular population, such as patients in a hospital or residents in a nursing home. The volunteer handler bringing the dog to visit is not providing a professional service but, rather, is following guidelines—established by the therapy dog organization the animal was evaluated by and by the facility being visited—to safely maximize naturalistic HAI benefits for the targeted population. In contrast, social workers and other health care professionals, working within the scope of professional practice, may do goal-directed work with an animal and a client or primary HAI beneficiary within the context of a therapeutic intervention to enhance the therapeutic value of that intervention. This may occur through having a volunteer handler with an animal (belonging to the volunteer handler) being present during portions of therapy as part of the therapy team. Alternately, the animal may reside with the professional who, within the scope of professional practice, is including the animal as part of the treatment team to help facilitate a client's goals. Using one's own animal as a therapy animal entails a dual role issue that must be proactively managed. For example, one's own animal is likely a beloved companion and family member who is simultaneously functioning as a therapeutic partner during a counseling session. When using one's own animal as a therapy animal, the social worker must be very intentional about focusing on therapeutic aspects of the animal's interactions with a client. Such animal-assisted goal-directed work within the scope of a social worker's professional practice should be documented and evaluated as part of a client's treatment plan.

Certifications and Practice Standards to Guide Training or Involvement of Animals in Therapeutic Roles

Such deliberate involvement of an animal by a health or human service professional within provision of professional treatment services is consistent with the definition of AAT provided by Animal Assisted Intervention International (AAII), a widely recognized international nonprofit organization seeking to establish standards, standardize terminology, and provide resources for animal-related interventions. In their online glossary, AAII uses the following terms to differentiate types of HAI that are conducted to convey benefits to humans:

- **Animal Assisted Therapy (AAT):** An AAT intervention is formally goal-directed and designed to promote improvement in physical, social, emotional and/or cognitive functioning of the person(s) involved and in which a specially trained animal-handler team is an integral part of the treatment process. AAT (Animal Assisted Therapy) is directed and/or delivered by a health/human service professional with specialized expertise and within the scope of practice of his/her profession. AAT may be provided in a variety of settings, may be group or individual in nature and may be implemented for persons of any age. There are specific goals for each individual involved and the process is documented and evaluated. (AAII, n.d., para. 2)

- **Animal Assisted Education (AAE):** An AAE is formally goal-directed and designed to promote improvement in cognitive functioning of the person(s) involved and in which a specially trained animal-handler team is an integral part of the educational process. AAE (Animal Assisted Education) is directed and/or delivered by an educational professional with specialized expertise and within the scope of practice of his/her profession. AAE may be provided in a variety of settings, may be group or individual in nature and may be implemented for persons of any age. There are specific goals for each individual involved and the process is documented and evaluated. (AAII, n.d., para. 3)

- **Animal Assisted Activity (AAA):** An AAA intervention is less goal-directed as specific objectives may not be planned. AAA (Animal Assisted Activity) is provided in a variety of settings, may be group or individual in nature and may be implemented for persons of any age. The AAA practitioners and/or animal handlers all are specially trained by an organization and meet the minimum standards set forth by AAII. Teams who provide AAA may also participate in Animal Assisted Therapy (AAT) or Animal Assisted Education (AAE) when the team is working directly with a healthcare, social service provider or with an educational practitioner. (AAII, n.d., para. 4)

AAII uses the umbrella term "animal-assisted intervention" (AAI) to broadly encompass all of the above terms and provides free booklets containing standards of practice for each of these AAI areas, available for download on their Web site (http://www.aai-int.org/aai/standards-of-practice/). Animals that engage in AAA, AAE, or AAT typically must pass an evaluation from a recognized therapy dog certification organization such as Pet Partners or Therapy Dogs International; this is covered in more detail in the Therapy Dogs section of this chapter. Dogs that are task trained and provide active assistance to ameliorate a person's disability must have training beyond that needed to perform the types of AAI described in the preceding paragraph. Task-trained dogs fall under the purview of Assistance Dogs International (ADI), which provides accreditation for programs that train such dogs and standards of practice for the various types of task training (ADI, n.d.-a).

Practice standards and certification involving horses in therapeutic roles generally fall under horse-specific organizations. As cited in Kruger and Serpell (2010, pp. 34–35), the following entities exemplify such organizations:

> the North American Riding for the Handicapped Association (NARHA), its subsection the Equine Facilitated Mental Health Associate (EFMHA), and its affiliate partner the American Hippotherapy Association, which provide the following separate definitions for the terms equine-facilitated psychotherapy (EFP) and hippotherapy:
>
> - EFP is an experiential psychotherapy that includes equine(s). It may include, but is not limited to, a number of mutually respectful equine activities such as handling, grooming, longeing (or lunging), riding, driving, and vaulting. EFP is facilitated by a licensed, credentialed mental health professional working with an appropriately credentialed equine professional. EFP may be facilitated by a mental health professional that is dually credentialed as an equine professional (EFMHA, 2003). EFP denotes an ongoing therapeutic relationship with clearly established treatment goals and objectives developed by the therapist in conjunction with the client. The therapist must be an appropriately credentialed mental health professional to legally practice psychotherapy and EFP.
> - Hippotherapy is done by an Occupational, Physical and Speech Therapist (OT, PT, ST) who has been specially trained to use the movement of the horse to facilitate improvements in their client/patient.

Legal Protections Pertaining to Public Access for Animals in Therapeutic Roles

Legal protections for animals engaged in therapeutic roles vary widely. Animals—generally dogs and, in some instances, miniature ponies or other species—may be task trained to provide active assistance to a person with a disability; these animals have the most extensive legal public access protections. Only animals who are trained to do tasks or provide active assistance to an individual with a disability meet the legal definition of service animal. As noted on the U.S. Department of Justice, Civil Rights Division (2011), Web site, there are also species limitations, in that only dogs may be defined as service animals. There are also provisions for miniature horses who provide task-trained assistance; to date, only dogs and miniature horses are addressed by the Americans with Disabilities Act (ADA) with regard to protected public access (U.S. Department of Justice, Civil Rights Division, 2011).

As of March 2011, the ADA gave the following definition of service dogs:

Service animal means any dog that is individually trained to do work or perform tasks for the benefit of an individual with a disability, including a physical, sensory, psychiatric, intellectual, or other mental disability. Other species of animals, whether wild or domestic, trained or untrained, are not service animals for the purposes of this definition. The work or tasks performed by a service animal must be directly related to the individual's disability. Examples of work or tasks include, but are not limited to, assisting individuals who are blind or have low vision with navigation and other tasks, alerting individuals who are deaf or hard of hearing to the presence of people or sounds, providing non-violent protection or rescue work, pulling a wheelchair, assisting an individual during a seizure, alerting individuals to the presence of allergens, retrieving items such as medicine or the telephone, providing physical support and assistance with balance and stability to individuals with mobility disabilities, and helping persons with psychiatric and neurological disabilities by preventing or interrupting impulsive or destructive behaviors. The crime deterrent effects of an animal's presence and the provision of emotional support, well-being, comfort, or companionship do not constitute work or tasks for the purposes of this definition. (Nondiscrimination on the Basis of Disability in Public Accommodations and Commercial Facilities, 2010)

With regard to public access for service dogs, according to the Web site of the U.S. Department of Justice, Civil Rights Division, the ADA requires

> government agencies, businesses, and non-profit organizations (covered entities) that provide goods or services to the public to make "reasonable accommodations" in their policies, practices, or procedures when necessary to accommodate people with disabilities. The service animal rules fall under this general principle. Accordingly, entities that have a "no pets" policy generally must modify the policy to allow service animals into their facilities. (U.S. Department of Justice, Civil Rights Division, 2015, para. 2)

The U.S. Department of Justice, Civil Rights Division (2011), offers a free publication that provides guidance on public service access for service animals titled *ADA Revised Requirements: Service Animals*. In this publication, specific rules pertaining to service dogs and public access are explained:

- Under the ADA, service animals must be harnessed, leashed, or tethered, unless these devices interfere with the service animal's work or the individual's disability prevents using these devices. In that case, the individual must maintain control of the animal through voice, signal, or other effective controls. (U.S. Department of Justice, Civil Rights Division, 2011, Service Animals Must Be Under Control section)
- When it is not obvious what service an animal provides, only limited inquiries are allowed. Staff may ask two questions: (1) is the dog a service animal required because of a disability, and (2) what work or task has the dog been trained to perform. Staff cannot ask about the person's disability, require medical documentation, require a special identification card or training documentation for the dog, or ask that the dog demonstrate its ability to perform the work or task.
- Allergies and fear of dogs are not valid reasons for denying access or refusing service to people using service animals. When a person who is allergic to dog dander and a person who uses a service animal must spend time in the same room or facility, for example,

in a school classroom or at a homeless shelter, they both should be accommodated by assigning them, if possible, to different locations within the room or different rooms in the facility.

- A person with a disability cannot be asked to remove his service animal from the premises unless: (1) the dog is out of control and the handler does not take effective action to control it or (2) the dog is not housebroken. When there is a legitimate reason to ask that a service animal be removed, staff must offer the person with the disability the opportunity to obtain goods or services without the animal's presence.

- Establishments that sell or prepare food must allow service animals in public areas even if state or local health codes prohibit animals on the premises.

- People with disabilities who use service animals cannot be isolated from other patrons, treated less favorably than other patrons, or charged fees that are not charged to other patrons without animals. In addition, if a business requires a deposit or fee to be paid by patrons with pets, it must waive the charge for service animals.

- If a business such as a hotel normally charges guests for damage that they cause, a customer with a disability may also be charged for damage caused by himself or his service animal.

- Staff are not required to provide care or food for a service animal. (U.S. Department of Justice, Civil Rights Division, 2011, Inquiries, Exclusions, Charges, and Other Specific Rules Related to Service Animals section)

Additional federal laws related to public access and animals in therapeutic roles include the definition of "assistance animal" under the Fair Housing Act (FHA) and the definition of "service animal" under the Air Carrier Access Act (ACAA); the ADA definition does not affect the broader definitions found in the FHA and ACAA (U.S. Department of Justice, Civil Rights Division, 2011), as each applies to specific types of public access. Specifically, the FHA and ACAA expand public access on a limited basis to be inclusive of animals who are not task trained to provide active assistance to a person with a disability but who are providing documented naturalistic or passive assistance that reduces the symptoms or impairment of a person with a mental disability. Hence, such animals may be permitted in no-pet housing as a housing accommodation and may also travel on airplanes with the person as a disability accommodation. To access no-pet housing and commercial air flights with an animal providing such support, the handler typically needs documentation to establish that the animal is an ESA; this is covered in detail in the ESAs section of this chapter.

Some state laws and local laws may define service animals (and the subsequent public access that is permitted) more broadly than the federal laws do. To determine whether such laws may be in place in a given state, one can contact the attorney general's office for that state.

Specific Therapeutic Roles

Combinations of these five differentiating factors identified by Parenti et al. (2013) result in specific, identifiable therapeutic roles of animals involved in providing HAI benefits. These roles are service animals, therapy animals, visitation animals, and ESAs. Each of these therapeutic roles for animals entails varying differences in the nature of the therapeutic support provided, the training needed by the animal, the attributes of the animal's primary handler, the certification and standards to guide training and practice related to an animal's therapeutic role, and legal allowances for public access for an animal in a therapeutic role. Table 9.1 delineates how each of these aspects relates to specific therapeutic roles of animals.

Service Dogs

Task-trained dogs are dogs who are extensively trained to complete specific tasks that actively mitigate symptoms or effects of a person's disability. As previously noted, there is not concordance in the legal terms used to describe such task-trained dogs, and the terms "service animal" and "assistance animal" are often used interchangeably in everyday conversations. However, the "service dog" is a legal term per ADA law and pertains to animals who have been task trained to perform actions that reduce symptoms or impairment of a person's disability. The meaning of "service dog" is currently not consistent across federal laws pertaining to

Table 9.1: Dimensions of Formal Therapeutic Roles of Animals

Therapeutic Role	Training	Nature of Assistance	Handler Attributes	Primary Beneficiary	Standards	Public Access Laws
Emotional support animal	None	Naturalistic, passive	Primary beneficiary	Handler	Verification letter	FHA, ACAA
Visitation dog	Therapy dog evaluation	Naturalistic, passive	Volunteer (AAA)	Persons inter-acted with	Therapy dog certification	Family specific
Therapy dog	Therapy dog evaluation	Naturalistic, passive	Professional (AAT)	Clients interacted with	Therapy dog certification	Family specific
Service dog	Extensive	Task orientated, active	Primary beneficiary	Handler	ADI, varies	ADA, FHA, ACAA

Notes: AAA = animal-assisted activity; AAT = animal-assisted therapy; ADI = Assistance Dogs International; FHA = Fair Housing Act; ACAA = Air Carrier Access Act; ADA = Americans with Disabilities Act.

Source: Adapted from "A Revised Taxonomy of Assistance Animals," by L. Parenti, A. Foreman, B. J. Meade, and O. Wirth, 2013, *Journal of Rehabilitation Research and Development, 50,* pp. 745–756.

public access for task-trained dogs. The FHA uses the term "assistance animals" to encompass both animals who provide task-trained assistance and animals who provide naturalistic or passive support that is necessary to mitigate distress and impairment related to a person's disability. The ACAA uses the term "service animal" but more broadly defines "service animal" to include animals that provide task-trained or innate (that is, naturalistic or passive) support needed to ameliorate distress and impairment related to a person's disability (Guidance Concerning Service Animals in Air Transportation, 2003, p. 24875). To summarize, both the FHA and the ACAA provide limited public access for animals who provide naturalistic or passive support to ameliorate symptoms and impairments of disability, whereas ADA law strictly limits their definition of service animals to dogs and, in some instances, miniature horses who are task trained.

Inconsistent terminology is also used across dog task-training entities. ADI refers to task-trained dogs as "assistance dogs" and delineates three types: guide dogs for individuals with visual impairments, hearing dogs for individuals with hearing impairments, and service dogs for people with disabilities other than those related to vision or hearing (ADI, n.d.-b). Service Dog Central, a prominent online community of "service dog partners and trainers working together to bring you our combined knowledge about service dogs" (Service Dog Central, n.d.-b, para. 1), refers to task-trained dogs as "service dogs" and identifies the following types of service dogs: guide dogs, hearing dogs, mobility dogs, seizure alert or response dogs, psychiatric service dogs, and autism dogs (Service Dog Central, n.d.-a). Because ADA law pertains to public access for task-trained dogs and uses the term "service dogs" to describe them, we have chosen to likewise use the term "service dog" in our book while acknowledging that numerous terms are used in practice to describe task-trained dogs.

A service dog's human handler is the person living with a disability and the primary beneficiary of HAI benefits through the animal's trained performance of task assistance. Individuals seeking a service dog may use private training or may apply through local or regional organizations that train service dogs to be matched with a dog that can complete specific tasks to ameliorate specific disabilities. Standards for task-trained service animals and service animal training are provided by ADI (n.d.-a). An example of a regional organization that trains service dogs is the nonprofit program Assistance Dogs for Achieving Independence (ADAI), which provides task-trained service dogs to assist people with mobility-related disabilities who live within a 250-mile radius of northwest Ohio (Ability Center of Greater Toledo, n.d.).

Social workers can help clients obtain service dogs through referrals to organizations such as ADAI. The types of task-trained assistance a dog can perform vary widely, depending on what is needed to assist a person who is living with a particular disability. An individual with a disability who is seeking a service dog through an organization must typically commit to completing a training program to learn to work with the dog so they can function as a team. For instance, at ADAI, human–dog teams complete an intensive final two-week training together at the ADAI facility. Follow-up visits are then scheduled at intervals to support and monitor how the person and dog work together, as well as to check on the animal's well-being. Additional information about the types of tasks dogs can be trained to do to assist with disabilities can be found online at Service Dog Central (n.d.-a).

Therapy Dogs

Therapy dogs, in contrast, do not perform specific tasks to ameliorate aspects of a disability. Rather, therapy dogs are typically very well-trained in general obedience and provide naturalistic support—conveying benefits of HAI through interactions and presence—to individuals in public settings such as nursing homes, clinics, or schools. Therapy dogs are typically credentialed when they pass a rigorous evaluation conducted by an evaluator from a national therapy dog credentialing organization such as Pet Partners (https://petpartners.org/) or Therapy Dogs International (http://www.tdi-dog.org/); organizations such as ADAI may also credential therapy dogs. Specific training is not required to have a dog evaluated by a national therapy dog organization; however, many of the evaluation tasks that must be performed by the dog are encompassed in the Canine Good Citizen Test administered by the American Kennel Club. Canine Good Citizen obedience classes are widely offered and can help to prepare a dog for a therapy dog evaluation. Information about the Canine Good Citizen test can be found online on the American Kennel Club Web site (American Kennel Club, n.d.).

The role of the handler is very important in determining whether a credentialed therapy dog is performing AAT or an AAA such as visiting with residents at a nursing home. As noted earlier in this chapter, AAT entails goal-directed, intentional incorporation of interaction with the therapy dog in the provision of professional interventions by a social worker or other health care worker; the purpose of the HAI in this context is to augment or enhance the benefit of the professional therapy service being provided, hence the term "animal-assisted therapy." A social worker may, on a volunteer basis, bring the same therapy dog to a particular setting (for example, a hospital, school, or nursing home) to convey HAI benefits through naturalistic interaction, performing an AAA. During AAA, explicit professional treatment is *not* being provided; however, the therapy dog is providing comfort and support to vulnerable individuals through its presence and interaction. Parenti et al. (2013) referred to such animals as "visitation animals." It is important to note that national dog therapy credentialing groups such as Pet Partners and Therapy Dogs International provide insurance related to AAA only, so, for example, the insurance provides coverage only when the therapy dog is doing visits with a volunteer handler on a volunteer basis, and no professional treatment or services are being delivered within the HAI. In contrast, when a social worker is including an animal as a therapeutic partner within the scope of professional practice or service delivery with a client, malpractice insurance that covers AAT should be in place (either individually, for those in private practice, or through an agency's insurance if the social worker is employed at an agency).

Another variation of AAA (or AAT) may occur through the work of residential facility dogs; again, such animals are typically credentialed as therapy dogs, and differentiating their AAA versus AAT therapeutic contributions to human well-being is best understood by considering the attributes of their human handlers. A facility therapy dog who resides in a group home and is working with a social worker conducting a therapy group at that group home would be participating in AAT. The same therapy dog might later in the same day be interacting more informally with group home residents and a volunteer facilitator during a craft activity; during such an interaction, the dog would be participating in an AAA.

For social workers seeking to incorporate AAIs within their practice, the *Handbook on Animal-Assisted Therapy: Theoretical Foundations and Guidelines for Practice* edited by Aubrey Fine (2010) is an excellent resource.

The University of Denver Graduate School of Social Work (n.d.) offers a comprehensive animal-assisted social work certificate, which is the first of its kind in the United States; the certificate program provides extensive training in AAIs as well as other aspects of HAI. More information about this certificate program is available online. Local, regional, and national conferences feature continuing education training on AAI; national organizations such the Animals and Society Institute list such events on their calendar, viewable online at http://www.animalsandsociety.org/events/. The New York City Chapter of the NASW has a special interest group named Social Workers Advancing the Human-Animal Bond; this group has monthly meetings and an active electronic mailing list that disseminates continuing education opportunities on a wide range of HAI topics, including AAT; more information about Social Workers Advancing the Human-Animal Bond can be viewed online at http://swahab.org/index .html. NASW Ohio is in the process of forming an HAI interest group.

ESAs

In contrast to service dogs, who are specifically trained to perform particular tasks related to reducing impairment that is due to an individual's disability, ESAs are animals whose therapeutic value occurs inherently within the context of the everyday relationship and interactions between the animal and a person with a mental disability. The person living with the mental disability is the primary beneficiary of benefits related to HAI derived from an ESA. ESAs do not receive any particular training to convey the physical, social, emotional, and psychological benefits of HAIs and HABs. Although these benefits can and are conveyed to a wide range of individuals in the general population, such benefits can be helpful in mitigating particular effects of a mental disability, hence the recognition of ESAs. An ESA is essentially a companion animal who is legally recognized as providing naturalistic or passive support that is needed to ameliorate the symptoms or impairments of a mental disability. ESAs have no special training to provide such support other than being socialized and generally well-behaved as a companion animal. It is the recognition of the therapeutic impact of the HAI benefits—described in detail in chapter 3 of this book—on a person's mental disability that distinguishes an ESA from a companion animal, not characteristics of the animal.

Reviewing some of the benefits of HAI can be useful in illuminating how ESAs are therapeutic without having specific training. A stress-mediation physical response can occur when a person strokes an animal; this entails the release of the feel-good hormone oxytocin, reductions in the stress-related hormones adrenalin and cortisol, reductions in heart and respiration rates, and a subsequent sense of feeling good. This stress-mediation response is beneficial for a person who does not have a mental health disability. For a person living with a mental health–related disability who has symptoms exacerbated by stressors, the stress-mediation response can significantly improve a person's ability to function. An animal is not trained in any particular way to evoke the stress-mediation response; rather, it occurs naturally through interactions with the animal. Reduction in symptoms through the stress-mediation response is just one of the potential ways an animal may, through everyday interactions, reduce impairment or improve functioning for an individual living with a mental health disability. In a review of existing studies of individuals with chronic mental illness who reported living with a companion animal or pet, a sense of emotional connectedness emerged as the most frequent HAI benefit self-reported by participants across studies (Hoy, 2014). Responsibility and self-efficacy were likewise represented across these identified studies; examples of quotes included multiple statements from individuals who reported at some point wanting to commit suicide but refraining because they felt responsible for their companion animals (Hoy, 2014).

When the clinical need for the companion animal and the therapeutic effect of the companion animal on a person's mental health disability are recognized and documented, the companion animal can be legally considered an ESA, with limited public access. The Michigan Animal Legal and Historical Center at Michigan State University explains the establishment of an ESA as follows:

> An emotional support animal is a companion animal that provides therapeutic benefit to an individual with a mental or psychiatric disability. The person seeking the emotional support animal must have a verifiable disability (the reason cannot just be a need for companionship). . . . The animal is viewed as a "reasonable accommodation" under the Fair Housing Amendments Act of 1988 (FHA or FHAct) to those housing communities that

have a "no pets" rule. In other words, just as a wheelchair provides a person with a physical limitation the equal opportunity to use and enjoy a dwelling, an emotional support animal provides a person with a mental or psychiatric disability the same opportunity to live independently. Most times, an emotional support animal will be seen as a reasonable accommodation for a person with such a disability. Failure to make reasonable accommodations by changing rules or policies can be a violation of the FHA unless the accommodation would be an undue financial burden on the landlord or cause a fundamental alteration to the premises. (Wisch, 2015)

Because ESAs are not task trained to provide assistance or support, they fall outside of ADA law related to public access for animals in therapeutic roles. However, both the ACAA and the FHA include access protections for animals who provide needed naturalistic or passive support for people living with disabilities. As explicated by the FHA:

> Both the Fair Housing Act and Section 504 require that in order to qualify as a reasonable accommodation, the requester must have a disability, and there must be a relationship between the requested accommodation and that person's disability. . . . Moreover, emotional support animals do not need training to ameliorate the effects of a person's mental and emotional disabilities. Emotional support animals by their very nature, and without training, may relieve depression and anxiety, and/or help reduce stress-induced pain in persons with certain medical conditions affected by stress. (Pet Ownership for the Elderly and Persons With Disabilities, 2008, p. 63836)

Hence, a person who has an ESA may not be prohibited from having the ESA in no-pets housing, as the ESA is treated as a reasonable accommodation under the FHA; because the animal is an ESA and not a pet, pet fees and deposits should not apply.

The ACAA delineates similar requirements for documentation related to ESAs:

> With respect to an animal used for emotional support (which need not have specific training for that function), airline

personnel may require current documentation (*i.e.*, not more than one year old) on letterhead from a mental health professional stating (1) that the passenger has a mental health-related disability; (2) that having the animal accompany the passenger is necessary to the passenger's mental health or treatment or to assist the passenger (with his or her disability); and (3) that the individual providing the assessment of the passenger is a licensed mental health professional and the passenger is under his or her professional care. Airline personnel may require this documentation as a condition of permitting the animal to accompany the passenger in the cabin. The purpose of this provision is to prevent abuse by passengers that do not have a medical need for an emotional support animal and to ensure that passengers who have a legitimate need for emotional support animals are permitted to travel with their service animals on the aircraft. Airlines are not permitted to require the documentation to specify the type of mental health disability, *e.g.*, panic attacks. (Guidance Concerning Service Animals in Air Transportation, 2003, p. 24876)

The ACAA's documentation requirements for ESAs offer useful guidelines for social workers who may be asked to document an ESA for a client. Although it may be tempting to provide ESA documentation for a client experiencing financial hardship, thus enabling the client to waive pet fees and deposits, it is not ethical. To meet the legal criteria for an ESA, the client must have a mental impairment that is mitigated by necessary naturalistic or passive support provided by the animal. Ideally, the ESA would be included as a strength, support, or resource in treatment and intervention plans and be an ongoing aspect of intervention focus. In instances where housing accommodations are denied for the ESA, a social worker may be called to court to verify the appropriateness of the ESA designation. It is crucial that the HAI benefits conveyed by the animal are explicitly linked to the mitigation or improvement of aspects of the client's mental disability; this should be noted as appropriate within assessments, case notes, treatment plans, and any ESA verification letters. To recap, using the ACAA requirements and other ESA-related laws, ESA verification letters should

- be on agency or professional letterhead
- clearly state that the client has a mental health–related disability
- clearly state that having the animal is necessary to the client's mental health or treatment because the animal reduces impairment or improves functioning related to the disability
- identify the individual providing the ESA documentation as a licensed mental health professional and the passenger as a client under his or her professional care
- be as current as possible (not more than one year old for ACAA purposes)

Unfortunately, many people abuse the privileges conveyed with ESA documentation. Numerous online services offer, for a fee, to provide ESA verification letters or certificates that enable a buyer to avoid housing or airline fees. This is highly unethical and creates barriers and public skepticism toward those who truly need their ESAs to mitigate aspects of a mental health disability. It is imperative that, as social workers, we hold ourselves to a high standard of integrity in the designation of ESAs and speak out against such abuses.

Ethical Concerns Related to Animals in Therapeutic Roles

As members of a value-driven profession, social workers need to be cognizant of the range of ethical implications regarding the use of animals for therapeutic purposes. Perhaps at the core of these concerns is the overarching question of whether humans should be using animals as tools. Taylor, Fraser, Signal, and Prentice (2016) suggested that the therapeutic roles of animals can be beneficial for both humans and animals. Social workers working with animals involved in AAIs need to be cognizant and proactive in adhering to AAI-related ethical principles to safeguard the well-being of the animals and people. In chapter 4 of this book, we list specific signs of stress that may be exhibited by dogs in therapeutic roles. It is crucial that social workers be familiar with both species-specific and individual animal–specific signs of stress to recognize and protect the animal's well-being. Animals who are stressed are more vulnerable to illness and may also exhibit behavioral issues. Serpell et al. (2010) offered the following ethical guidelines in working with animals in AAIs:

- All animals utilized therapeutically must be kept free from abuse, discomfort, and distress, both physical and mental.
- Proper health care for the animal must be provided at all times.
- All animals should have access to a quiet place where they can have time away from their work activities. Clinicians must practice preventative health procedures for all animals.
- Interactions with clients must be structured so as to maintain the animal's capacity to serve as a useful therapeutic agent.
- Only the most compelling of human needs (e.g., avoiding serious mental or physical injury) should ever be allowed to take precedence over the basic needs of the animal. (p. 502)

ADI (2014) also has ethical standards relating to task-trained dogs. Task-training dog organizations must follow these ethical standards to be accredited by ADI.

Conclusion

Human well-being can be greatly enhanced through HAI with animals in a range of therapeutic roles, such as ESAs, visitation animals, therapy animals, and service animals. Understanding the dimensions of these roles will help social workers to better assist their clients in accessing and maximally benefiting from such HAI-related support. Social workers need to be aware of and responsive to both human and animal needs in therapeutic interactions; such interventions need not only benefit humans, as they are not either-or scenarios. The TAHS Therapeutic Pet Visitation Program, as described in chapter 10 of this book, exemplifies a program in which both humans and animals benefit tremendously. Through this program, individuals residing at nursing homes and other care facilities receive HAI-related benefits through interactions with temperament-tested, health-checked shelter animals during supervised visits of the animals to the facilities; the shelter animals simultaneously receive socialization, environmental enrichment, and increased adoption visibility. As stated by Taylor et al., ethical application of AAIs within social work practice necessitates consideration of well-being for both the animal and the human involved:

> Sufficient care, pre-planning and resources are needed to ethically engage the services of animals in social work activities. Well-meaning but misdirected actions may involve any type of animal and any cohort of people. Naïve actions, such as giving rabbits/guinea pigs to young children, and simply hoping no harm comes to the animals, are not acceptable. Similarly problematic would be for social workers to help adopt cats or dogs without helping them think through the longer-term implications, or failing to support clients' care for their animals, post-adoption. . . . Enthusiasm for the benefits animals can bring to clients' lives needs to be tempered with sensible and sensitive concerns for the partner animals. Knowledge about the species and the individual animals involved in the programs is essential. Good intentions but insufficient skills and expertise in animal handling will not suffice. . . . We caution against the vast proliferation of AATs driven solely by human concerns. (Taylor et al., 2016, pp. 147–148)

Emerging Specialties: Veterinary Social Work and Social Work Practice at Humane Societies

While sitting in a waiting room in veterinary specialty clinic with her cat, Hamlet, Janet observed an elderly woman come out of the door from the clinic exam area. She was clasping with both hands a small red collar with a tag on it, and her face was streaked with tears. The woman paused and looked around the crowded waiting area, which had fallen silent except for an anxiously whining dog, and then walked, quietly sobbing, through the waiting area to the parking lot. On reaching her car, she leaned hunched over the trunk and continued to sob. Hamlet's name was then called for his examination. Janet asked the veterinary staff holding Hamlet's chart about available support for the woman and was told veterinary staff had talked with her during her appointment, reviewed options for her pet's body, and given her a number to call for pet loss support group information. The woman had apparently come without another person to the appointment; glancing around, Janet realized that most of the people in the waiting room were likewise by themselves with their animals. While helpful steps had been taken, it was clear that additional on-site supports for the woman would have been beneficial, such as when social work and chaplain services are offered in human hospitals after the death of a patient. The basic premise of this book is that HAI is relevant across a wide spectrum of social work practice settings and populations; however, specialty practice settings for social workers in which the focus is explicitly related to HAI are emerging, such as within veterinary hospitals and humane societies.

Currently, numerous veterinary hospitals across the United States have a social worker on staff. The University of Tennessee offers a veterinary social work program and runs an annual international conference on the practice of veterinary social work. Just as medical social work was developed and integrated into the flow of hospital and outpatient care, veterinary social work recognizes and addresses the interdependent relationships between veterinary medical providers, clients, patients (companion animals), family members, and other social supports. Veterinary social workers may also function as employee assistance providers to veterinary staff who face high levels of burnout and compassion fatigue and as instructors in veterinary colleges who teach interpersonal communication and crisis skills to veterinary students. Similar opportunities are emerging for social workers to practice at humane societies in various capacities, such as promoting shelter staff wellness, reducing compassion fatigue, facilitating grief support groups, managing pet visitation programs in which shelter pets visit nursing facilities, coordinating companion animal sheltering programs for individuals who are fleeing domestic violence or are otherwise displaced from their homes, overseeing mobile meal programs for housebound individuals who have companion animals, and collaborating with other community entities in developing needed human–animal support services. Within this chapter, we discuss these cutting-edge areas of social work practice related to HAI.

Social Work in Veterinary Settings

According to Laetitia Clayton of *NASW News*, "social workers who are animal lovers might find that veterinary social work offers the best of both worlds" (Clayton, 2013, para. 1). Clayton described veterinary social work as an emerging field and shared interview excerpts from a conversation with Elizabeth Strand, director of veterinary social work at the University of Tennessee in Knoxville. The University of Tennessee offers a certificate program that trains MSW students in veterinary social work; Michigan State University and other social work schools provide field placements and training in veterinary social work. According to Strand, the focus of veterinary social work is "on tending to human needs that arise in relationships with animals and maintaining the values of the social work profession" (Clayton, 2013, para. 13). From the perspective of a veterinarian, Goldberg (2015) likewise summarized the scope of veterinary social work practice as attending to the human needs that arise from HAI within a veterinary context. Strand coined the term "veterinary social work" and identified four areas within it: grief and pet loss, animal-assisted interactions, the link between human and animal violence, and compassion fatigue management.

Veterinary social workers have two primary human client systems: (1) human clients who bring their animals to veterinary clinics for services and (2) veterinary medical and support staff. Although the animal patients are a core component of the therapeutic triad (Pierce, 2015) comprising human clients, animal patients, and veterinary staff, the current veterinary social work scope of practice focuses explicitly on addressing human needs. Veterinary social workers provide employee assistance–related services for veterinary medical and support staff to prevent or reduce compassion fatigue and increase health and wellness. Additional services offered by veterinary social workers include but are not limited to grief and pet loss counseling, AAIs, and assistance in addressing the link between human and animal violence. When a veterinary social worker is part of a vet clinic team, veterinary staff can request social work consults as needed to explicitly address clients' emergent psychosocial concerns. Veterinary staff can thus focus more fully on the provision of veterinary medical services without struggling to simultaneously address clients' psychosocial issues. Through this use of social work expertise, workplace stress experienced by veterinary staff related to difficult client situations can be reduced. For instance, a veterinary social worker can provide emotional and grief support for human clients agonizing over difficult decisions such as euthanasia for an ailing pet or help coordinate with animal abuse and child abuse investigators when abuse or neglect concerns arise. In many ways, the veterinary social worker functions as an integral part of an interprofessional team, much like a medical social worker works within interprofessional teams at hospitals and outpatient clinics. However, the veterinary social worker may also assume employee assistance responsibilities for the veterinary clinic staff.

Veterinary Social Work: Grief and Pet Loss

Veterinary social workers provide support to both clients and veterinary staff related to end-of-life decision making, grief, and pet loss. As discussed in chapter 8 of this book, the loss of a companion animal to death can occur in a variety of ways, for example, suddenly and unexpectedly owing to an accidental trauma or acute illness or through euthanasia after a prolonged illness or decline. Although veterinary professionals are highly trained in the provision of medical treatment for animals, the emotional reactions and psychosocial stressors faced by human clients caring for ill animals are challenges uniquely suited to social work practitioners. Human grief related to pet loss is complex and multifaceted. Making end-of-life care decisions for a beloved animal, including when or whether to euthanize an animal, can be an extremely difficult for a client.

In providing end-of-life decision-making support to clients of veterinary practices, the veterinary social worker works closely with the treating veterinarian and explores and addresses the following with clients: medical prognosis and quality-of-life issues for the animal, palliative care versus treatment, personal beliefs about euthanasia, and practical considerations such as financial and home care resources (J. Nielsen, personal communication, November 2, 2013). Client support during such difficult times can be maximized through interprofessional collaboration between the veterinarian and veterinary social workers. The veterinarian formulates a medical prognosis, provides treatment and palliative or hospice care options, and illuminates quality-of-life considerations for an animal patient. The veterinary social worker can, through active supportive listening and sharing of quality-of-life assessment tools, facilitate client decision making around care options and quality-of-life considerations so that the client makes choices that are congruent with that client's values, resources, and means and that minimize the suffering of the animal patient.

The International Association of Animal Hospice and Palliative Care published transdisciplinary guidelines and considerations to support both human clients and animal patients. The guidelines target the following areas: pain, suffering, and animal well-being; ethical and legal aspects of palliative care for animals and their caregivers; mental health considerations for animal hospice caregivers; care for the animal patient at the end of life; and methods of supporting the animal's caregiver in providing animal hospice nursing (Shanan et al., 2014). As with other types of social work, a key concept in the provision of transdisciplinary veterinary hospice services is the plan of care; the guidelines call for the establishment of "an individualized, comprehensive, and transdisciplinary plan of care for each animal patient and care-giving family. The plan of care is based on a clear understanding of caregiver expectations and goals for the animal's care before, during, and after death" (Shanan et al., 2014, p. 6).

Quality-of-life assessments can be an invaluable tool offered by veterinary social workers to support clients in end-of-life decision making. The International Association of Animal Hospice and Palliative Care guidelines state the following regarding quality-of-life assessment:

> Quality of life assessments involve a collaborative effort among veterinarians, other animal hospice team members, and caregivers, and rely on careful observation of an animal. They encourage us to ask "what is important to this animal in his or her life?" and to remember that each individual animal has unique likes and dislikes. For example, loss of mobility might negatively impact a dog who loves to play ball and Frisbee more significantly that it would a dog whose favorite activity is sleeping in a sunny spot under a window. Individual animals also have unique capacities to adapt to change. A disabled animal may continue to enjoy his or her favorite activities if creatively modified to fit the animal's condition. A disabled animal may also develop "new" favorite activities. Quality of life assessments track important behaviors over time; and should provide a written record that can guide discussions about care options and facilitate finding consensus on end-of-life decisions. . . .
>
> Some popular quality of life assessment tools use a numerical scoring system. . . . While tools like this can be a good guide, it may be necessary for caregivers to weigh some factors like respiratory distress and severe pain more heavily than other factors like incontinence or the inability to play catch. (Shanan et al., 2014, pp. 10–11)

The Association for Pet Loss and Bereavement (n.d.-b) offers such a numerical assessment scale in the resource section of their Web page— the Quality of Life Scale (Villalobos, 2011)—which asks pet caregivers to score animal patients using a scale of 0 to 10 (10 being ideal) in the following areas: hurt, hunger, hydration, hygiene, happiness, mobility, and more good days than bad. The scale indicates that a total over 35 points represents acceptable life quality to continue with pet hospice.

If clients so choose, veterinary social workers can be present to offer support during the euthanasia process. Although veterinarians administering the procedure typically give a detailed, step-by-step explanation to prepare clients for what to expect, including possible reactions an animal may have (for example, bowel evacuation, muscle twitching, eyes not closing), veterinary social workers can provide additional support and education about what to expect during the process and help to ensure that clients' questions and concerns are fully addressed. Some veterinary facilities offer dedicated "comfort rooms" in which euthanasia takes place; home or outdoor euthanasia may also be a desirable option for the client. Payment and signing of paperwork should be done beforehand whenever possible so the client can be free to react and exit without dealing with additional tasks (J. Nielson, personal communication, November 2, 2013).

Veterinary social workers may also be asked to assist with conversations with children regarding the death of a companion animal or to provide resources to assist parents and caregivers in supporting their children. This may be the first experience with death for many children. As when dealing with human death, children have age-related developmental stages that mediate their responses to death. The Association for Pet Loss and Bereavement (n.d.-a) has explicit resources and guidelines for supporting children during the death of companion animals available on their Web site. Their online resources include a detailed outline of age-related developmental stages related to companion animal death, a list of questions a child may ask, ways for children to memorialize their animals, a list of suggested others to inform (such as teachers or other caregivers), and a bibliography page of children's books on the death of a beloved animal (Association for Pet Loss and Bereavement, n.d.-a).

As detailed in chapter 8 on loss within this book, grief related to animal loss may emerge in many ways and is related to a variety of factors, such as attachment to the animal and type of death. Having a veterinary social worker available to consult when an animal dies allows for immediate professional support. According to Joelle Nielson (personal communication, November 1, 2015), Ohio State University Veterinary Medical Center social worker and Honoring the Bond Program coordinator, suicide risk assessment and crisis intervention are regular aspects of her work with clients who have lost companion animals. In addition to on-site crisis support, referrals to grief support and professional counseling can be facilitated as needed by the veterinary social worker. The experience of disenfranchised grief can also be mitigated through offering a memorial ceremony in which the loss of a beloved companion animal is acknowledged and honored. Nielson (personal communication, November 2, 2013) organizes the Annual Companion Animal Remembrance Ceremony, which has occurred annually at the Ohio State Veterinary Medical Center since 2009. The Honoring the Bond Web site described this ceremony as follows:

> The typical agenda for the ceremony includes short speeches from a variety of people about loss and the celebration of the lives of our lost companion animals. We show a slideshow that includes photos that have been submitted by owners that will attend the ceremony. We also offer a personal remembrance at our Remembrance Tree area, located on east side of the Veterinary Medical Center. The first three years, owners placed hearts on the tree. The last two years, we wanted something a little more permanent. Owners wrote their pet's name and optionally, some words, on a stone/marker, and placed [it] under the tree. After the personal remembrances at the tree, many owners choose to stay for an additional activity in which we make a keepsake to take with us. . . . Owners have talked about this part being a nice way to actually talk with others that are experiencing similar feelings about their loss. It is a nice way for owners to share their special memories about the lives of their companions that are no longer with us. (Ohio State University Veterinary Medical Center, Hospital for Companion Animals, n.d.)

Aftercare decisions and grief support are likewise areas where the professional expertise of the veterinary social worker is used. Determining what to do with the deceased animal's body with regard to cremation or burial and considering how to memorialize one's animal can be difficult and painful. Veterinary social workers can provide much-needed support in the identification and exploration of related options and resources.

Veterinary Social Work: Compassion Fatigue Management

As discussed in chapter 4, veterinary staff, like animal protection workers, are at risk of compassion fatigue. In addition to providing support to human clients, veterinary social workers may also provide linkage or direct support services to veterinary professionals and students to aid in managing compassion fatigue, secondary trauma, and stress. As stated by registered veterinary technician Dobbs (2012),

> You sit in a chair, listening to a person across the room talk about the horrible accident she witnessed. Through her tears, she describes the vehicle, the scene as it happened in slow-motion, the way her beloved family member's body looked after being struck.
>
> In this scenario, you could be a social worker or counselor, trying to absorb your client's story while avoiding becoming emotionally involved in the situation as it unfolds in words in front of you—trying to avoid the post-traumatic stress that is part of your job day in and day out as you witness peoples' worst nightmares happening in real life.
>
> Now, you look in the mirror and you are wearing scrubs.
>
> The beloved family member, Fluffy, lies in back on a table while the team tries to revive the animal that has been hit by a car right in front of your client.
>
> Nothing prepared you for this part of the job as a veterinary professional, the intense tales of trauma, illness, even abuse and neglect.
>
> You walk out of the room fighting the urge to cry. Nowhere do you remember reading that being a veterinary technician meant reliving horrible moments with pet owners. (paras. 1–6)

To recap, compassion fatigue is, according to Dr. Charles Figley, director of the Tulane Traumatology Institute, "a state experienced by those helping people or animals in distress; it is an extreme state of tension and preoccupation with the suffering of those being helped to the degree that it can cause a secondary traumatic stress for the helper" (Figley, n.d., para. 1).

Fortunately, the trend is shifting in veterinary education toward pro-actively equipping veterinary professionals with interpersonal, crisis, and self-care skills. Veterinary social workers employed by veterinary colleges may provide classroom instruction to veterinary students focused on building interpersonal and crisis skills along with direct support to students and faculty through counseling, coaching, and linking to ongoing supports as needed. The Bayer Animal Health Communication Project is a nonprofit organization that provides training and online resources to strengthen communication skills among veterinarians, veterinary technicians, and other members of the veterinary team. Ohio State University veterinary social worker Joelle Nielson (personal communication, November 2, 2013) stated that Bayer's materials are invaluable in the veterinary education process, and the content is routinely used in didactics with veterinary students. Veterinary social workers who have a primary focus on employee and student assistance to veterinary professionals would benefit from reviewing Bayer's 12 online educational modules, which are available free of charge, focus on specific aspects of communication within veterinary practice, and address the following 12 topics (Bayer Animal Health Communication Project, n.d.):

- building successful teams
- eliciting and understanding the client's perspective
- dealing with roles and choices in decision making with clients
- guiding clients through difficult decisions about euthanasia
- enhancing client adherence to treatment
- communicating nonverbally with clients
- navigating difficult interactions between veterinarians and clients
- handling money issues in the veterinary–client relationship
- recognizing ethical issues with clients and crisis care
- disclosing medical errors
- communicating within the veterinary health care team

Veterinary social workers may also help to organize and promote wellness and prevention activities for veterinary staff in veterinary settings. The 2015 Veterinary Wellness and Social Work Summit conference compiled a resource manual of wellness-focused activities that can be readily implemented in veterinary practice settings. For example, the Ohio State University Veterinary Medical Center has Wellness Wednesdays, during which a variety of wellness-focused activities are offered free of charge for students, faculty, and staff. As part of these activities, therapy dogs visit and interact with students, faculty, and staff to help relieve stress and boost morale. (Note that although AAI is identified as a component of veterinary social work practice, it is treated in detail in this book in chapter 9.)

Veterinary Social Work: The Link between Human and Animal Violence

As delineated in chapter 6 in this book, where we discuss HAI and violence, "the link" refers to the overlap between violence toward animals and violence toward people. Although the mandated reporting responsibilities of social workers, including veterinary social workers, are generally clearly understood with regard to vulnerable humans, reporting requirements with regard to animals who are abused or neglected are less clear. The therapeutic triad in veterinary medicine includes the human client, the animal patient, and the veterinary professional; however, the question of where the veterinary professional's loyalty ought ultimately to be—with the human client or the animal patient—has yet to be resolved (Pierce, 2015). Veterinary social workers, by joining the interprofessional and transdisciplinary veterinary team, likewise become a part of this therapeutic system and the ethical quandaries therein. Chapter 4 in this book details the social work profession's ethical responsibilities related to reporting animal abuse and neglect. However, when practicing social work within a veterinary social work context, it is important to note that veterinarians have differing reporting responsibilities that vary vastly by the state in which the veterinarian is providing services. Veterinarians are mandated reporters of animal abuse in 17 states, permitted to report animal abuse in 18 states, and forbidden to report animal abuse in the state of Kentucky (Arkow, 2015b). Veterinary social workers following the guidance in the NASW *Code of Ethics* regarding their responsibilities to the larger society and the need to protect vulnerable others from harm may find themselves in conflict with veterinary professionals on their teams who have restrictive laws related to animal abuse reporting. To address this conflict, veterinary social workers can proactively develop clear reporting policies and protocols, with professional legal and ethical obligations specified and spelled out, to enable an effective response to suspected animal abuse. The National Link Coalition has extensive resources for veterinary and other professionals, such as manuals describing how to respond to suspected cruelty and neglect in veterinary practice, a guidebook on the veterinary profession's role in preventing family violence, a veterinary animal welfare tool kit, and a sample protocol for reporting animal abuse. These and many other resources can be viewed at the National Link Coalition resource materials Web page: http://nationallinkcoalition.org/resources/articles-research.

Social Work in Humane Societies

Historical Context

The practice of social work within a humane society setting may not, at first glance, seem to be a logical fit; however, social work tasks and functions were historically handled in part by humane society entities. For instance, the first child abuse cruelty conviction was accomplished through collaboration between a church worker and the ASPCA. In 1873, a church worker discovered a 10-year-old girl who showed signs of abuse and neglect; because no child protection entities existed at the time, the worker turned to Henry Bergh, founder of the ASPCA, to document the abuse and prepare a legal petition to initiate the removal of the child from the abusive circumstances (Watkins, 1990). The 1884 annual report of the TAHS for the Prevention of Cruelty to Animals and Children gave an explicit reference to addressing such needs of abused and neglected children:

> A large number of complaints have been received charging parents or guardians with using undue severity in correcting their children. The admonitions of the Agent have usually sufficed to prevent a repetition. Thirty-seven children have been taken by the Society from homes and influences which were rapidly degrading them, or from inhumane parents or guardians, and placed. (p. 16)

In the 10th annual report of the TAHS (1894), three separate departments—the Department of Children, the Department of Animals, and the Department of Associated Charities (one of the Toledo community's precursors to United Way)—are described; two of the three departments primarily focused on human well-being. This annual report also detailed the use of "friendly visitors" to reach out to and support individuals living in poverty; this friendly visitor approach is congruent with early social work casework strategies:

The increasing tide of poverty in cities can be arrested and materially diminished by systematic and persistent friendly visitation. By this method, each family may be reached by a person of experience, whose talent is best adapted to its special need. The plan is to select a volunteer friend for each family. The difficulty from which the family suffers forms the medium of a friendly acquaintance, which is continued without limit. Their peculiar troubles are considered and means of relief are pointed out, supplemented when necessary by personal efforts and the aid of others whose sympathy may be enlisted. The object of this work is to teach the poor better methods of living. To cultivate self-respect, self-reliance, and independence. (TAHS, 1894, p. 35)

Although the responsibility for delivering human services has since migrated to separate human-focused organizations and missions, many aspects of humane society work remain highly relevant to social work practice. The TAHS, in collaboration with the University of Toledo Social Work Program, has provided MSW internships since 2010. Contemporary social work practice within humane society settings has vast applications for alleviating suffering and promoting well-being for humans and animals.

MSW Internships at the TAHS

In 2010, the first two advanced MSW internship placements were developed through collaboration between the University of Toledo social work program and TAHS leaders. Using iterations of collaborative, consensus-building strategies at several planning meetings, the following questions were mutually identified as important, explored, and delineated:

- What is a social worker and what does a social worker do?
- What are the needs and goals of the humane society that could be addressed by an MSW intern?
- How could the humane society meet the social work program learning objectives and competencies as a field site?
- How would the students be supervised?

Through these brainstorming and planning meetings, University of Toledo and TAHS stakeholders identified three current areas of need that an MSW intern could address: developing and implementing an ESA placement program, assessing and intervening to reduce compassion fatigue among TAHS staff, and developing strategies to improve community awareness of and responses to the link between violence toward people and violence toward animals. Two specific advanced MSW internships were created to address these areas.

One of the MSW internships focused primarily on mental health–related practice. Specifically, this internship focused on addressing staff compassion fatigue and collaborating with a community mental health center to develop and coordinate an ESA placement program known as Hope and Recovery Pet (HARP). A private donor provided lifetime funding for food, supplies, and veterinary services for TAHS animals placed as ESAs with adults living with serious mental illness who were referred by the mental health center to participate in the HARP program. The HARP program has thrived through collaborative efforts between community mental health staff, the University of Toledo social work program, and TAHS staff. ProMedica, a nonprofit regional health care system in northwest Ohio and southeast Michigan, is currently partnering to expand and build on the HARP program within its service system. To our knowledge, the HARP program is the first ESA placement program in the United States.

Like many service professionals working with vulnerable populations, staff at humane societies like TAHS are at risk of compassion fatigue (Rogelberg et al., 2007). Animal shelter work involves exposure to animals who are ill, abused, neglected, or unwanted, as well as to the people responsible for the animals' being in such states. Euthanasia is also a routine aspect of animal sheltering work. Such experiences can be extremely difficult and emotionally draining for those who undertake such work to help animals and thus can result in compassion fatigue (Rogelberg et al., 2007) among animal shelter staff. At the mezzo level, the MSW intern focused on mental health, working with TAHS staff to enhance staff well-being and achieve organizational goals related to compassion fatigue reduction. Subsequent MSW interns have continued to build on the wellness aspect of this placement, which has culminated in the development of an annual Wellness Week for TAHS staff for the past two years. Staff provide feedback on areas of concern and self-care that they are interested in, and the MSW intern develops an array of activities that target these areas, such as massages (donated by community providers) and stress management tips from the TAHS employee assistance provider, for each day of Wellness Week. Daily lunches for participating TAHS staff are donated by community restaurants.

The second MSW internship focused primarily on using the advanced generalist social work model to strengthen community responsiveness toward violence by (a) assessing overlap and differences between child abuse investigation and animal cruelty investigation, (b) creating and implementing educational programming for cruelty investigators and child abuse staff to increase their ability to collaborate across systems, and (c) working to increase community awareness of the link between violence toward animals and violence toward humans (Ascione & Shapiro, 2009). Because this intern had years of experience as a child abuse investigator before he entered the MSW program and internship placement, he was uniquely suited to initiate connections between TAHS and area human protection entities. The MSW intern shadowed the TAHS animal cruelty investigators and quickly identified similarities between the families he encountered in his child abuse work role and the families he encountered in his TAHS internship role. By engaging with TAHS and the local child abuse investigation organization, the intern was able to establish a liaison role to facilitate and expedite cross reporting between the agencies, ultimately strengthening the local safety net for both children and animals at risk. The intern also collaborated with the TAHS executive director to conduct cross-reporting training for the county child protection agency and did a related presentation at a regional antiviolence coalition meeting.

The responsibilities of subsequent MSW placements at TAHS have further expanded to include coordination of the TAHS Therapeutic Pet Visitation program. Through this program, temperament-tested (by the TAHS on-staff behaviorist), vet-checked shelter animals are taken to over 30 nursing homes and other care facilities in northwest Ohio to visit with facility residents. The MSW intern conducts some of the visits with shelter animals and also assists with recruiting, training, and coordinating the TAHS volunteers who also provide visits. These visits offer the individuals residing at facilities opportunities to experience the benefits of HAI, as delineated in chapter 3 of this book, while simultaneously providing additional enrichment, socialization, and potential adoption exposure for the shelter animals. The TAHS Therapeutic Pet Visitation program exemplifies how therapeutic programs can benefit both the humans and the animals who are involved. TAHS also offers other human–animal relationship supports for vulnerable persons, such as a mobile meals program that delivers free animal food to housebound individuals, foster home placements for individuals leaving domestic violence situations, and numerous animal-assisted education initiatives such as a children's program for reading to shelter animals.

Although human service and animal protection organizations are largely separate entities, connections between animal well-being and human well-being remain salient and relevant in contemporary society. The TAHS MSW internships described in this chapter encompass only some of the opportunities for social work practice at a humane society. For instance, additional focuses could be development of an animal hoarding task force, creation and facilitation of a pet loss grief support group, and expansion of other human–animal relationship support services. Humane societies are settings in which connections between human welfare, animal welfare, and service delivery can be explicitly addressed through social work practice.

CONCLUSION

Exciting areas of social work practice explicitly focused on aspects of HAI and the HAB are currently emerging. The need to address the relevance of HAI and the HAB in clients' lives, however, spans the tremendous range of social work practice settings and populations. HAI, as a potential strength or stressor for a given client system, should be routinely assessed for across areas of social work practice. Omitting the relevance of companion animals in the lives of clients from social work practice can preclude effective incorporation of an existing strength (for example, the ability to connect with and care for a companion animal) or resource (the companionship or social support derived from a companion animal) within a given client system (Netting et al., 1987). Conversely, such an omission may also preclude the identification of a client stressor or barrier; for instance, a client may be experiencing disenfranchised grief as a result of the death of a cherished companion animal (Chur-Hansen et al., 2010; Doka, 2002) or may be unwilling to leave an abusive relationship because she or he does not wish to leave a companion animal behind, given that most shelters do not permit companion animals (Walton-Moss et al., 2005). Within this book, we sought to highlight and summarize many areas of HAI that are relevant for social work practice and to offer practical suggestions for how such areas can be incorporated into everyday social work practices. We recognize that many of the topics we addressed could easily be expanded into separate books; these topics warrant much additional consideration and exploration. It is our sincere hope that this book will provide a basic understanding of why and how to routinely address various dimensions of HAI and the HAB within social work practice. By doing so, our profession can ultimately better support the well-being of both humans and animals.

REFERENCES

Ability Center of Greater Toledo. (n.d.). Need a dog. Retrieved October 20, 2016, from http://www.abilitycenter.org/we-can-help/programs/assistance-dogs/our-dogs/need-a-dog/

Akiyama, H., Holtzman, J. M., & Britz, W. E. (1987). Pet ownership and health status during bereavement. *OMEGA—Journal of Death and Dying, 17,* 187–193.

Albert, A., & Bulcroft, K. (1988). Pets, families, and the life course. *Journal of Marriage and the Family, 50,* 543–552.

Allen, K., Blascovich, J., & Mendes, W. B. (2002). Cardiovascular reactivity and the presence of pets, friends, and spouses: The truth about cats and dogs. *Psychosomatic Medicine, 64,* 727–739.

Allen, K. M., Blascovich, J., Tomaka, J., & Kelsey, R. M. (1991). Presence of human friends and pet dogs as moderators of autonomic responses to stress in women. *Journal of Personality and Social Psychology, 61,* 582–589.

American Kennel Club. (n.d.). *About Canine Good Citizen.* Retrieved from http://www.akc.org/dog-owners/training/canine-good-citizen/about/

American Pet Products Association. (2015). *Pet industry market size & ownership statistics* [Press release]. Retrieved from https://american-petproducts.org/press_industrytrends.asp

American Psychiatric Association. (2013). *Diagnostic and statistical manual of mental disorders* (5th ed.). Arlington, VA: Author.

American Veterinary Medical Association. (2001). A community approach to dog bite prevention. *Journal of the American Veterinary Medical Association, 218,* 1732–1749.

American Veterinary Medical Association. (2014). *Cross-reporting of animal and child abuse.* Retrieved from https://www.avma.org/Advocacy/StateAndLocal/Pages/sr-animal-abuse-cross-reporting.aspx?PF=1

American Veterinary Medical Association. (n.d.). *The human-animal interaction and human-animal bond* [Policy]. Retrieved from https://www.avma.org/KB/Policies/Pages/The-Human-Animal-Bond.aspx

Anderson, W. P., Reid, C. M., & Jennings, G. L. (1992). Pet ownership and risk factors for cardiovascular disease. *Medical Journal of Australia, 157,* 298–301.

Animal Assisted Intervention International. (n.d.). Animal assisted intervention. Retrieved from http://www.aai-int.org/aai/animal-assisted-intervention/

Antonacopoulos, N.M.D., & Pychyl, T. A. (2010). An examination of the potential role of pet ownership, human social support and pet attachment in the psychological health of individuals living alone. *Anthrozoös, 23,* 37–54. doi:10.2752/175303710X12627079939143

Archer, J. (2000). Sex differences in aggression between heterosexual partners: A meta-analytic review. *Psychological Bulletin, 126,* 651–680. doi:10.1037/0033-2909.126.5.651

Arkow, P. (2014). Form of emotional blackmail: Animal abuse as a risk factor for domestic violence. *Family & Intimate Partner Violence Quarterly, 7,* 7–13.

Arkow, P. (2015a). Animal therapy on the community level: The impact of pets on social capital. In A. H. Fine (Ed.), *Handbook on animal-assisted therapy: Foundations and guidelines for animal-assisted interventions* (4th ed., pp. 43–51). San Diego: Elsevier Academic Press. doi:10.1016/B978-0-12-801292-5.00005-5

Arkow, P. (2015b, November). *Practice guidance for the effective response by veterinarians to suspected animal cruelty, abuse and neglect.* Paper presented at the Veterinary Wellness and Social Work Summit, Knoxville, TN.

Arkow, P., Boyden, P., & Patterson-Kane, E. (2011). *Practical guidance for the effective response by veterinarians to suspected animal cruelty, abuse and neglect.* Schaumburg, IL: American Veterinary Medical Association.

Ascione, F. R. (1993). Children who are cruel to animals: A review of research and implications for developmental psychopathology. *Anthrozoös, 6,* 226–247. doi:10.2752/089279393787002105

Ascione, F. R. (1997). Battered women's reports of their partners' and their children's cruelty to animals. *Journal of Emotional Abuse, 1*(1), 119–133.

Ascione, F. R., & Arkow, P. (1999). *Child abuse, domestic violence, and animal abuse: Linking the circles of compassion for prevention and intervention.* West Lafayette, IN: Purdue University Press.

Ascione, F. R., & Peak, T. (with McDonald, S., & Clark, L.). (2009, October). *Animal welfare issues and elder adult maltreatment: A national study*. Poster session presented at the International Society for Anthrozoology/Human Animal Interaction International Conference, Kansas City, MO. Retrieved from https://portfolio.du.edu/downloadItem/206240

Ascione, F. R., & Shapiro, K. (2009). People and animals, kindness and cruelty: Research directions and policy implications. *Journal of Social Issues, 65,* 569–587. doi:10.1111/j.1540-4560.2009.01614.x

Ascione, F. R., Weber, C. V., Thompson, T. M., Heath, J., Maruyama, M., & Hayashi, K. (2007). Battered pets and domestic violence: Animal abuse reported by women experiencing intimate violence and by nonabused women. *Violence Against Women, 13,* 354–373. doi:10.1177/1077801207299201

Assistance Dogs International. (2014). *ADI minimum standards and ethics.* Retrieved from http://www.assistancedogsinternational.org/wp-content/uploads/2012/03/ADI_MINIMUM_STANDARDS ETHICS_08-2014.pdf

Assistance Dogs International. (n.d.-a). *Standards.* Retrieved from http://www.assistancedogsinternational.org/standards/

Assistance Dogs International. (n.d.-b). *Types of assistance dogs.* Retrieved from http://www.assistancedogsinternational.org/about-us/types-of-assistance-dogs/

Association for Pet Loss and Bereavement. (n.d.-a). *Children and pet loss.* Retrieved from http://www.aplb.org/support/children_and_pet_loss.php

Association for Pet Loss and Bereavement. (n.d.-b). *Quality of Life Scale.* Retrieved from http://www.aplb.org/resources/quality-of-life_scale.php

Asthma and Allergy Foundation of America. (n.d.). *Pet allergy: Are you allergic to dogs or cats?* Retrieved from http://www.aafa.org/page/pet-dog-cat-allergies.aspx

Barker, S. B., & Dawson, K. S. (1998). The effects of animal-assisted therapy on anxiety ratings of hospitalized psychiatric patients. *Psychiatric Services, 49,* 797–801.

Baun, M. M., & McCabe, B. W. (2003). Companion animals and persons with dementia of the Alzheimer's type: Therapeutic possibilities. *American Behavioral Scientist, 47,* 42–51. doi:10.1177/0002764203255211

Bayer Animal Health Communication Project. (n.d.). *Modules overview.* Retrieved from https://veterinarycommunication.org/modules/modulelanding.php

Beck, A. M. (1999). Companion animals and their companions: Sharing a strategy for survival. *Bulletin of Science, Technology & Society, 19,* 281–285. doi:10.1177/027046769901900404

Beetz, A., Uvnäs-Moberg, K., Julius, H., & Kotrschal, K. (2012). Psychosocial and psychophysiological effects of human-animal interactions: The possible role of oxytocin. *Frontiers in Psychology, 3,* Article 234. doi:10.3389/fpsyg.2012.00234

Benefit. (n.d.-a). In *The free dictionary.* Retrieved from http://www.the freedictionary.com/benefit

Benefit. (n.d.-b). In *Merriam-Webster's online dictionary.* Retrieved from http://www.merriam-webster.com/dictionary/benefit

Bentham, J. (1789). *An introduction to the principles of morals and legislation.* Oxford, England: Clarendon Press.

Bergamasco, L., Osella, M. C., Savarino, P., Larosa, G., Ozella, L., Manassero, M., et al. (2010). Heart rate variability and saliva cortisol assessment in shelter dog: Human–animal interaction effects. *Applied Animal Behaviour Science, 125,* 56–68. doi:10.1016/j .applanim.2010.03.002

Berget, B., Ekeberg, Ø., & Braastad, B. O. (2008). Animal-assisted therapy with farm animals for persons with psychiatric disorders: Effects on self-efficacy, coping ability and quality of life, a randomized controlled trial. *Clinical Practice and Epidemiology in Mental Health, 4,* Article 9. doi:10.1186/1745-0179-4-9

Berry, C., Patronek, G., & Lockwood, R. (2005). Long-term outcomes in animal hoarding cases. *Animal Law, 11,* 167–194.

Bikales, G. (1975). The dog as "significant other." *Social Work, 20,* 150–152.

Boat, B. (2014). *The Childhood Trust Survey on Animal-Related Experiences: 10 screening questions for children, adolescents, and adults.* Retrieved from http://nationallinkcoalition.org/wp-content/uploads/2014/10/Barbara-Boat-CTSARE-Animal-Related-Experiences.pdf

Bowlby, J. (1969). *Attachment and loss: Vol. 1. Attachment.* New York: Basic Books.

Bowlby, J. (2005). *A secure base: Clinical applications of attachment theory.* Abington, United Kingdom: Taylor & Francis.

Brown, S. (2002). Ethnic variations in pet attachment among students at an American school of veterinary medicine. *Society & Animals, 10,* 249–266. doi:10.1163/156853002320770065

Brown, S. (2005). The under-representation of African Americans in animal welfare fields in the United States. *Anthrozoös, 18,* 98–121. doi:10.2752/089279305785594225

Carmack, B. J. (1991). The role of companion animals for persons with AIDS/HIV. *Holistic Nursing Practice, 5*(2), 24–31.

Carmack, B. J. (2003). *Grieving the death of a pet.* Minneapolis: Augsburg Books.

Carter, B. E., & McGoldrick, M. E. (1988). *The changing family life cycle: A framework for family therapy.* New York: Gardner Press.

Centers for Disease Control and Prevention. (n.d.-a). *Keeping pets healthy keeps people healthy too!* Retrieved from http://www.cdc.gov/healthy-pets/index.html

Centers for Disease Control and Prevention. (n.d.-b). *Proper hygiene when around animals.* Retrieved from http://www.cdc.gov/healthy-water/hygiene/etiquette/around_animals.html

Centers for Disease Control and Prevention. (n.d.-c). *Specific groups & settings.* Retrieved from http://www.cdc.gov/healthypets/specific-groups/index.html

Christensen, J. (2013, December 19). Therapy dogs: "Perfect medicine" to help students survive finals. *CNN.* Retrieved from http://www.cnn.com/2013/12/19/health/students-therapy-dogs

Chur-Hansen, A. (2010). Grief and bereavement issues and the loss of a companion animal: People living with a companion animal, owners of livestock, and animal support workers. *Clinical Psychologist, 14*(1), 14–21.

Clayton, L. (2013). Emerging field joins two professions. *NASW News.* Retrieved from https://www.socialworkers.org/pubs/news/2013/07/veterinary-social-work.asp

Cline, K. M. (2010). Psychological effects of dog ownership: Role strain, role enhancement, and depression. *Journal of Social Psychology, 150,* 117–131. doi:10.1080/00224540903368533

Colombo, G., Buono, M. D., Smania, K., Raviola, R., & De Leo, D. (2006). Pet therapy and institutionalized elderly: A study on 144 cognitively unimpaired subjects. *Archives of Gerontology and Geriatrics, 42,* 207–216.

Costin, L. B. (1991). Unraveling the Mary Ellen legend: Origins of the "cruelty" movement. *Social Service Review, 65*, 203–223.

Crocken, B. (1981). Veterinary medicine and social work: A new avenue of access to mental health care. *Social Work in Health Care, 6*(3), 91–94.

Cronley, C., Strand, E. B., Patterson, D. A., & Gwaltney, S. (2009). Homeless people who are animal caretakers: A comparative study. *Psychological Reports, 105*, 481–499.

Cummings School of Veterinary Medicine at Tufts University. (n.d.). *Crisis intervention, counseling and case management for Hoarding of Animals Research Consortium.* Retrieved from http://vet.tufts.edu/hoarding/crisis-intervention-counseling-and-case-management/

Cunningham, J. H., & Edelman, A. (2012, December 17). Comfort dogs help ease pain of mourning Newtown community. *New York Daily News.* Retrieved from http://www.nydailynews.com/news/national/comfort-dogs-helping-ease-pain-sandy-hook-tragedy-article-1.1222295

Davis, J. H. (1991). Pet ownership and stress over the family life cycle. *Holistic Nursing Practice, 5*(2), 52–57.

Dawson, S., & Campbell, B. (2009). Are we barking up the wrong tree? Questioning the appropriateness of human models for bereavement applied to the experience of companion animal loss by euthanasia. In A. Kasher (Ed.), *Dying, assisted death and mourning* (pp. 97–113). New York: Rodopi.

Dellinger, M. (2008). Using dogs for emotional support of testifying victims of crime. *Animal Law Review, 15*, 171–192.

DeMello, M. (2012). *Animals and society: An introduction to human-animal studies.* New York: Columbia University Press.

Diaconescu, M. (2015). Burnout, secondary trauma and compassion fatigue in social work. *Social Work Review/Revista De Asistenţă Socială, 14*(3), 57–63.

Digges, J. B. (2009). Human-companion animal social relationships. *Reflections: Narratives of Professional Helping, 15*(1), 35–41.

Dobbs, K. (2012). Fighting compassion fatigue in the veterinary industry. *Veterinary Practice News.* Retrieved from http://www.veterinarypracticenews.com/August-2012/Fighting-Compassion-Fatigue-In-The-Veterinary-Industry/

Doka, K. (2002). *Disenfranchised grief: New directions, challenges, and strategies for practice.* Champaign, IL: Research Press.

Doka, K. (Ed.). (2008). *Disenfranchised grief in historical perspective.* Washington, DC: American Psychological Association.

Endenburg, N., & van Lith, H. A. (2011). The influence of animals on the development of children. *Veterinary Journal, 190,* 208–214.

Errera, P., & Richmond, C. (1961). Is time so scarce? *Social Work, 6,* 96–100.

Faver, C. A. (2009). Seeking our place in the web of life: Animals and human spirituality. *Journal of Religion & Spirituality in Social Work: Social Thought, 28,* 362–378.

Faver, C. A. (2013). Environmental beliefs and concern about animal welfare: Exploring the connections. *Journal of Sociology and Social Welfare, 40,* 149–168.

Faver, C. A., & Cavazos, A. M., Jr. (2007). Animal abuse and domestic violence: A view from the border. *Journal of Emotional Abuse, 7*(3), 59–81. doi:10.1080/10926798.2007.10766832

Faver, C. A., & Cavazos, A. M., Jr. (2008). Love, safety, and companion-ship: The human-animal bond and Latino families. *Journal of Family Social Work, 11,* 254–271.

Faver, C. A., & Strand, E. B. (2003a). Domestic violence and animal cru-elty: Untangling the web of abuse. *Journal of Social Work Education, 39,* 237–253.

Faver, C. A., & Strand, E. B. (2003b). To leave or to stay? Battered women's concern for vulnerable pets. *Journal of Interpersonal Violence, 18,* 1367–1377. doi:10.1177/0886260503258028

Faver, C. A., & Strand, E. B. (2007). Fear, guilt, and grief: Harm to pets and the emotional abuse of women. *Journal of Emotional Abuse, 7*(1), 51–70.

Federal Bureau of Investigation. (2016). *Tracking animal cruelty: FBI col-lecting data on crimes against animals.* Retrieved from https://www .fbi.gov/news/stories/-tracking-animal-cruelty

Field, N. P., Nichols, C., Holen, A., & Horowitz, M. J. (1999). The relation of continuing attachment to adjustment in conjugal bereavement. Journal of Consulting and Clinical Psychology, *67,* 212–218.

Figley, C. (n.d.). *The Compassion Fatigue Awareness Project.* Retrieved from http://www.compassionfatigue.org/index.html

Fine, A. H. (Ed.). (2010). *Handbook on animal-assisted therapy: Theoretical foundations and guidelines for practice.* London: Academic Press.

Fine, A. H., & Beck, A. (2010). Understanding our kinship with animals: Input for health care professionals interested in the human/animal bond. In A. H. Fine (Ed.), *Handbook on animal-assisted therapy: Theoretical foundations and guidelines for practice* (pp. 3–16). London: Academic Press.

Fitzgerald, A. J. (2007). "They gave me a reason to live": The protective effects of companion animals on the suicidality of abused women. *Humanity & Society, 31,* 355–378.

Flynn, C. P. (2000). Woman's best friend: Pet abuse and the role of companion animals in the lives of battered women. *Violence Against Women, 6,* 162–177.

Flynn, C. P. (2011). Examining the links between animal abuse and human violence. *Crime, Law and Social Change, 55,* 453–468. doi:10.1007/s10611-011-9297-2

Freund, L. S., McCune, S., Esposito, L., Gee, N. R., & McCardle, P. (Eds.). (2016). *The social neuroscience of human–animal interaction.* doi:10.1037/14856-000

Friedmann, E., Katcher, A. H., Lynch, J. J., & Thomas, S. A. (1980). Animal companions and one-year survival of patients after discharge from a coronary care unit. *Public Health Reports, 95,* 307–312.

Frost, R., & Steketee, G. (2010). *Stuff: Compulsive hoarding and the meaning of things.* New York: Houghton Mifflin Harcourt.

Fujimura, K., Johnson, C., Ownby, D., Cox, M., Brodie, E., Havstad, S., et al. (2010). Man's best friend? The effect of pet ownership on house dust microbial communities. *Journal of Allergy and Clinical Immunology, 126,* 410–412. doi:10.1016/j.jaci.2010.05.042

Gern, J. E., Reardon, C. L., Hoffjan, S., Nicolae, D., Li, Z., Roberg, K. A., et al. (2004). Effects of dog ownership and genotype on immune development and atopy in infancy. *Journal of Allergy and Clinical Immunology, 113,* 307–314. doi:10.1016/j.jaci.2003.11.017

Gerwolls, M. K., & Labott, S. M. (1994). Adjustments to the death of a companion animal. *Anthrozoös, 7,* 172–187.

Goldberg, K. (2015, November). *The role of social workers within veterinary medicine: A veterinarian's perspective.* Paper presented at the Veterinary Wellness and Social Work Summit, Knoxville, TN.

Gorczyca, K., Fine, A. H., Venn-Watson, S., Nelson, L., Brooks, A., Lipp, J. L., et al. (2010). Human/animal support services: The evolution of the San Francisco model and pet-associated zoonoses education. In A. H. Fine (Ed.), *Handbook on animal assisted therapy: Theoretical foundations and guidelines for practice* (3rd ed., pp. 329–356). San Diego: Academic Press.

Guidance Concerning Service Animals in Air Transportation, 68 Fed. Reg. 24874, 24876 (May 2, 2003) (to be codified at 14 C.F.R. pt. 382).

Hall, P. L., & Malpus, Z. (2000). Pets as therapy: Effects on social interaction in long-stay psychiatry. *British Journal of Nursing, 9,* 2220–2225.

Handlin, L., Hydbring-Sandberg, E., Nilsson, A., Ejdebäck, M., Jansson, A., & Uvnäs-Moberg, K. (2011). Short-term interaction between dogs and their owners: Effects on oxytocin, cortisol, insulin and heart rate—an exploratory study. *Anthrozoös, 24,* 301–315. doi:10.27 52/175303711X13045914865385

Handlin, L., Nilsson, A., Ejdebäck, M., Hydbring-Sandberg, E., & Uvnäs-Moberg, K. (2012). Associations between the psychological characteristics of the human–dog relationship and oxytocin and cortisol levels. *Anthrozoös, 25,* 215–228. doi:10.2752/175303712X13316289505468

Hanrahan, C. (2011). Challenging anthropocentricism in social work through ethics and spirituality: Lessons from studies in human-animal bonds. *Journal of Religion & Spirituality in Social Work: Social Thought, 30,* 272–293.

Hardesty, J. L., Khaw, L., Ridgway, M. D., Weber, C., & Miles, T. (2013). Coercive control and abused women's decisions about their pets when seeking shelter. *Journal of Interpersonal Violence, 28,* 2617–2639.

Hogan, E. F., & Hoy, J. (2015, November). *Sage advice: Understanding client perspectives on end-of-life decision-making for companion animals.* Paper presented at the Veterinary Wellness and Social Work Summit, Knoxville, TN.

Holder, C. (2013). All dogs go to court: The impact of court facility dogs as comfort for child witnesses on a defendant's right to a fair trial. *Houston Law Review, 50,* 1155–1187.

Hollander, E. (2013). Social synchrony and oxytocin: From behavior to genes to therapeutics. *American Journal of Psychiatry, 170,* 1086–1089. doi:10.1176/appi.ajp.2013.13070848

Horowitz, S. (2008). The human–animal bond: Health implications across the lifespan. *Alternative and Complimentary Therapies, 14*(5), 251–256.

Horowitz, S. (2010). Animal-assisted therapy for inpatients: Tapping the unique healing power of the human–animal bond. *Alternative and Complimentary Therapies, 16*, 339–343. doi:10.1089/act.2010.16603

Hosey, G., & Melfi, V. (2014). Human-animal interactions, relationships and bonds: A review and analysis of the literature. *International Journal of Comparative Psychology, 27*, 117–142.

Hoy, J. (2014, January). *Companion animals as evokers of connection and responsibility among individuals with serious mental illness: A systematic review of qualitative findings.* Paper presented at the Society for Social Work and Research National Annual Conference, San Antonio, TX.

Hoy, J. (2016). *The Hope and Recovery Pet (HARP) program evaluation.* Unpublished manuscript.

Hoy, J., Delgado, M., Sloane, H., & Arkow, P. (in press). Rediscovering connections between animal welfare and human welfare: Developing master's level social work internships at a humane society. *Journal of Social Work.*

Humane Society of the United States. (n.d.). *Animal abuse and neglect.* Retrieved from http://www.humanesociety.org/issues/abuse_neglect/

Hurn, S. (2012). *Humans and other animals: Cross-cultural perspectives on human–animal interactions.* London: Pluto Press.

Hutton, J. S. (1998). Animal abuse as a diagnostic approach in social work: A pilot study. In R. Lockwood & F. R. Ascione (Eds.), *Cruelty to animals and interpersonal violence: Readings in research and application* (pp. 415–418). West Lafayette, IN: Purdue University Press.

Hutton, V. E. (2014). Companion animals and wellbeing when living with HIV in Australia. *Anthrozoös, 27*, 407–421.

Institute for Human-Animal Connection: History. (2016). Retrieved from http://www.du.edu/humananimalconnection/history.html

Johnson, T. P., Garrity, T. F., & Stallones, L. (1992). Psychometric evaluation of the Lexington Attachment to Pets Scale (LAPS). *Anthrozoös, 5*, 160–175.

Julius, H., Beetz, A., Kotrschal, K., Turner, D., & Uvnäs-Moberg, K. (2012). *Attachment to pets: An integrative view of human-animal relationships with implications for therapeutic practice.* Cambridge, MA: Hogrefe.

Kabel, A., Khosla, N., & Teti, M. (2015). The dog narratives: Benefits of the human–animal bond for women with HIV. *Journal of HIV/AIDS & Social Services, 14*, 405–416. doi:10.1080/15381501.2013.860069

Katcher, A., Friedmann, E., Beck, A., & Lynch, J. (1983).Talking, looking, and blood pressure: Physiological consequences of interaction with the living environment. In A. H. Katcher & A. M. Beck (Eds.), *New perspectives on our lives with companion animals* (pp. 351–359). Philadelphia: University of Pennsylvania Press.

Katz, J. (2004). *The new work of dogs: Tending to life, love, and the family.* New York: Random House.

Kidd, A. H., & Kidd, R. M. (1995). Children's drawings and attachment to pets. *Psychological Reports, 77,* 235–241. doi:10.2466/pr0.1995.77.1.235

Komorsky, D., & Woods, D. (2015, January). *A multi-method approach to examining California domestic violence shelter companion animal policies.* Paper presented at the Society for Social Work and Research National Conference, San Antonio, Texas.

Krause-Parello, C. A. (2008). The mediating effect of pet attachment support between loneliness and general health in older females living in the community. *Journal of Community Health Nursing, 25,* 1–14. doi:10.1080/07370010701836286

Krause-Parello, C. A. (2012). Pet ownership and older women: The relationships among loneliness, pet attachment support, human social support, and depressed mood. *Geriatric Nursing, 33,* 194–203. doi:10.1016/j.gerinurse.2011.12.005

Krause-Parello, C. A., & Friedmann, E. (2014). The effects of an animal-assisted intervention on salivary alpha-amylase, salivary immunoglobulin A, and heart rate during forensic interviews in child sexual abuse cases. *Anthrozoös, 27,* 581–590. doi:10.2752/089279314X14072268688005

Kruger, K., & Serpell, J. (2010). Animal-assisted interventions in mental health: Definitions and theoretical foundations. In A. H. Fine (Ed.), *Handbook on animal-assisted therapy: Theoretical foundations and guidelines for practice* (3rd ed., pp. 33–48). London: Academic Press.

Kurdek, L. A. (2009). Pet dogs as attachment figures for adult owners. *Journal of Family Psychology, 23,* 439–446. doi:10.1037/a0014979

Lee, S. A., & Surething, N. A. (2013). Neuroticism and religious coping uniquely predict distress severity among bereaved pet owners. *Anthrozoös, 26,* 61–76.

Levine, G. N., Allen, K., Braun, L. T., Christian, H. E., Friedmann, E., Taubert, K. A., et al. (2013). Pet ownership and cardiovascular risk: A scientific statement from the American Heart Association.

Circulation, 127, 2353–2363. Retrieved from http://circ.ahajournals. org/content/early/2013/05/09/CIR.0b013e31829201e1.full.pdf

Lizik, R. (n.d.). *The fatal epidemic of animal care workers that no one is talking about*. Retrieved from http://barkpost.com/compassion-fatigue-animal-workers/

Lockwood, R. (2002). *Making the connection between animal cruelty and the abuse and neglect of vulnerable adults*. Retrieved from http://nationallink coalition.org/wp-content/uploads/2013/01/ElderAbuse-Lockwood-.pdf

Lockwood, R., & Ascione, F. R. (Eds.). (1998). *Cruelty to animals and interpersonal violence: Readings in research and application*. West Lafayette, IN: Purdue University Press.

Lunghofer, L. (2016a). *Assessing children's relationships with animals* [Webinar]. Available from https://attendee.gotowebinar.com/ register/5218650894795268098

Lunghofer, L. (2016b). *Intervening with children who witnessed or engaged in animal abuse* [Webinar]. Available from https://attendee.gotowe binar.com/register/1614313240480492802

Lynch, C. A., Loane, R., Hally, O., & Wrigley, M. (2010). Older people and their pets: A final farewell. *International Journal of Geriatric Psychiatry, 25*, 1087–1088. doi:10.1002/gps.2469

Mallon, G. (1994). Cow as co-therapist: Utilization of farm animals as therapeutic aides with children in residential treatment. *Child and Adolescent Social Work Journal, 11*, 455–474.

Manor, W. (1991). Alzheimer's patients and their caregivers: The role of the human-animal bond. *Holistic Nursing Practice, 5*(2), 32–37.

Marr, C. A., French, L., Thompson, D., Drum, L., Greening, G., Mormon, J., et al. (2000). Animal-assisted therapy in psychiatric rehabilitation. *Anthrozoös, 13*, 43–47.

Mathieu, F. (2012). *The compassion fatigue workbook: Creative tools for transforming compassion fatigue and vicarious traumatization*. New York: Routledge.

Matsuoka, A., & Sorenson, J. (2013). Human consequences of animal exploitation: Needs for redefining social welfare. *Journal of Sociology and Social Welfare, 40*, 7–32.

Mayor's Alliance for NYC's Animals. (2015). *Sample pet information page*. Retrieved from http://www.helpingpetsandpeoplenyc.org/ sample-pet-information

Mayor's Alliance for NYC's Animals. (n.d.). *Domestic violence and pets*. Retrieved from http://www.helpingpetsandpeoplenyc.org/domestic-violence-and-pets/

McDonald, S. E., Ascione, F. R., Williams, J. H., & Brown, S. M. (2014, January). *Anxiety, depression, and post-traumatic stress among youth exposed to intimate partner violence: The impact of witnessing animal cruelty*. Paper presented at the 18th Annual Program Meeting of the Society for Social Work & Research, San Antonio, TX.

McGoldrick, M., Preto, N. G., & Carter, B. (2015). *The expanding family life cycle: Individual, family, and social perspectives* (5th ed.). Boston: Pearson.

McNicholas, J., & Collis, G. M. (2001). Children's representations of pets in their social networks. *Child: Care, Health and Development, 27*, 279–294. doi:10.1046/j.1365-2214.2001.00202.x

Mehelich, C. (2011). Compassion fatigue: Emotional burnout in the animal care field. *BellaDOG Magazine*. Retrieved from http://www.compassionfatigue.org/pages/belladog.pdf

Mehta, G. M. (1969). Use of domesticated birds and animals in a child guidance clinic. *Indian Journal of Social Work, 29*, 400–405.

Miller, D. H., & Ashmore, D. L. (1967). The ethology of social work. *Social Work, 12*, 60–68.

Mills, J. T., 3rd, & Yeager, A. F. (2012, April–June). Definitions of animals used in healthcare settings. *United States Army Medical Department Journal, 2012*, 12–17.

Miura, A., Bradshaw, J.W.S., & Tanida, H. (2002). Attitudes towards assistance dogs in Japan and the UK: A comparison of college students studying animal care. *Anthrozoös, 15*, 227–242. doi:10.2752/089279302786992496

Morley, C., & Fook, J. (2005). The importance of pet loss and some implications for services. *Mortality, 10*, 127–143. doi:10.1080/13576270412331329849

National Association of Social Workers. (2015). *Code of ethics of the National Association of Social Workers*. Retrieved from https://www.socialworkers.org/pubs/code/code.asp

National Association of Social Workers, New York City Chapter. (n.d.). *Social Workers Advance the Human Animal Bond interest group*. Retrieved October 12, 2016, from http://www.naswnyc.org/?185

Nett, R. J., Witte, T. K., Holzbauer, S. M., Elchos, B. L., Campagnolo, E. R., Musgrave, K. J., et al. (2015). Notes from the field: Prevalence of risk factors for suicide among veterinarians—United States, 2014. *Morbidity and Mortality Weekly Report, 64*(5), 131–132.

Netting, F. E., Wilson, C. C., & New, J. C., Jr. (1984). Developing a multidisciplinary pet placement program for community-based elderly. *Journal of Applied Gerontology, 3,* 181–191. doi:10.1177/073346488400300208

Netting, F. E., Wilson, C. C., & New, J. C. (1987). The human-animal bond: Implications for practice. *Social Work, 32,* 60–64.

Nondiscrimination on the Basis of Disability in Public Accommodations and Commercial Facilities, 28 C.F.R. § 36.104 (2010).

Odendaal, J.S.J., & Meintjes, R. A. (2003). Neurophysiological correlates of affiliative behaviour between humans and dogs. *Veterinary Journal, 165,* 296–301. doi:10.1016/S1090-0233(02)00237-X

Ohio State University Veterinary Medical Center, Hospital for Companion Animals. (n.d.). *Animal remembrance ceremony.* Retrieved from http://www.vet.osu.edu/vmc/companion/our-services/honoring-bond-support-animal-owners/remembrance-ceremony

Olmert, M. D. (2009). *Made for each other: The biology of the human-animal bond.* Cambridge, MA: Da Capo Press.

Packman, W., Carmack, B. J., Katz, R., Carlos, F., Field, N. P., & Landers, C. (2014). Online survey as empathic bridging for the disenfranchised grief of pet loss. *Omega (Westport), 69,* 333–356. doi:10.2190/OM.69.4.a

Packman, W., Carmack, B. J., & Ronen, R. (2011–2012). Therapeutic implications of continuing bonds expressions following the death of a pet. *Omega (Westport), 64,* 335–356.

Packman, W., Field, N. P., Carmack, B. J., & Ronen, R. (2011). Continuing bonds and psychosocial adjustment in pet loss. *Journal of Loss and Trauma, 16,* 341–357.

Parenti, L., Foreman, A., Meade, B. J., & Wirth, O. (2013). A revised taxonomy of assistance animals. *Journal of Rehabilitation Research and Development, 50,* 745–756.

Parish-Plass, N. (2008). Animal-assisted therapy with children suffering from insecure attachment due to abuse and neglect: A method to lower the risk of intergenerational transmission of abuse? *Clinical Child Psychology and Psychiatry, 13*(1), 7–30. doi:10.1177/1359104507086338

Peak, T., Ascione, F., & Doney, J. (2012). Adult protective services and animal welfare: Should animal abuse and neglect be assessed during adult protective services screening? *Journal of Elder Abuse & Neglect, 24,* 37–49.

Pet Ownership for the Elderly and Persons With Disabilities, 73 Fed. Reg. 63,834, 63836 (Oct. 10, 2008) (to be codified at 24 C.F.R. pt. 5).

Pets Are Wonderful Support. (2009). *The healing power of the human-animal bond: A guide to starting a HASS (human-animal support services) organization in your community.* Retrieved from http://www.shanti.org/paws_pdf/paws_start_up_kit.pdf

Pets Are Wonderful Support. (n.d.-a). *About us.* Retrieved from http://www.shanti.org/pages/paws_about_us.html

Pets Are Wonderful Support. (n.d.-b). *Overview of client services.* Retrieved from http://www.shanti.org/pages/paws_client_services.html

Phillips, A. (2012). *Sheltering Animals & Families Together (SAF-T Program) start-up manual.* Retrieved from http://alliephillips.com/wp-content/uploads/2010/11/SAF-T-Start-Up-Manual-2012.pdf

Pierce, J. (2015, November). *The last walk: Caring for our companion animals at the end of life.* Paper presented at the Veterinary Wellness and Social Work Summit, Knoxville, TN.

Planchon, L. A., Templer, D. I., Stokes, S., & Keller, J. (2002). Death of a companion cat or dog and human bereavement: Psychosocial variables. *Society & Animals, 10,* 93–105.

Podberscek, A. L. (2009). Good to pet and eat: The keeping and consuming of dogs and cats in South Korea. *Journal of Social Issues, 65,* 615–632. doi:10.1111/j.1540-4560.2009.01616.x

Pomeroy, E., & Garcia, R. (2008). *The grief assessment and intervention workbook: A strengths perspective.* Belmont, CA: Brooks/Cole.

Prichard, D. (2012). *Dogs take a bite out of dental office anxiety.* Retrieved from http://www.speareducation.com/spear-review/2012/12/dogs-take-a-bite-out-of-dental-office-anxiety/#.VG6iQ2wo7oY

Prosser, L., Townsend, M., & Staiger, P. (2008). Older people's relationships with companion animals: A pilot study. *Nursing Older People, 20*(3), 29–32. doi:10.7748/nop2008.04.20.3.29.c6496

Putney, J. M. (2013). Relational ecology: A theoretical framework for understanding the human-animal bond. *Journal of Sociology & Social Welfare, 40*(4), 57–80.

Putney, J. M. (2014). Older lesbian adults' psychological well-being: The significance of pets. *Journal of Gay & Lesbian Social Services, 26,* 1–17. doi:10.1080/10538720.2013.866064

Quackenbush, J. E. (1981). Pets, owners, problems and the veterinarian: Applied social work in a veterinary teaching hospital. *Compendium on the Continuing Education for the Small Animal Practitioner, 3,* 764–765.

Quackenbush, J. E., & Glickman, L. (1984). Helping people adjust to the death of a pet. *Health & Social Work, 9,* 42–48.

Raina, P., Waltner-Toews, D., Bonnett, B., Woodward, C., & Abernathy, T. (1999). Influence of companion animals on the physical and psychological health of older people: An analysis of a one-year longitudinal study. *Journal of the American Geriatrics Society, 47,* 323–329. doi:10.1111/j.1532-5415.1999.tb02996.x

Reed, L. (2000). The importance of companion animals in social work assessments. *Animals Today, 8*(2), 22.

Reevy, G. M., & Delgado, M. M. (2014). Are emotionally attached companion animal caregivers conscientious and neurotic? Factors that affect the human–companion animal relationship. *Journal of Applied Animal Welfare Science, 18,* 239–258. doi:10.1080/10888705.2014 .988333

Rehn, T., Handlin, L., Uvnäs-Moberg, K., & Keeling, L. J. (2014). Dogs' endocrine and behavioural responses at reunion are affected by how the human initiates contact. *Physiology & Behavior, 124,* 45–53.

Rehn, T., Lindholm, U., Keeling, L., & Forkman, B. (2014). I like my dog, does my dog like me? *Applied Animal Behaviour Science, 150,* 65–73. doi:10.1016/j.applanim.2013.10.008

Rew, L. (2000). Friends and pets as companions: Strategies for coping with loneliness among homeless youth. *Journal of Child and Adolescent Psychiatric Nursing, 13,* 125–140.

Rigdon, J. D., & Tapia, F. (1977). Children who are cruel to animals: A follow-up study. *Journal of Operational Psychiatry, 8,* 27–36.

Risley-Curtiss, C. (2010). Social work practitioners and the human–companion animal bond: A national study. *Social Work, 55,* 38–46.

Risley-Curtiss, C. (2013). Expanding the ecological lens in child welfare practice to include other animals. *Journal of Sociology & Social Welfare, 40*(4), 107–130.

Risley-Curtiss, C. (2014). *Children and Animals Together Assessment and Intervention Program*. Retrieved from http://psychweb.cisat.jmu.edu/graysojh/pdfs/Volume101-CATProg%20Desc_updated%201-2014.pdf

Risley-Curtiss, C., Holley, L. C., Cruickshank, T., Porcelli, J., Rhoads, C., Bacchus, D.N.A., & Murphy, S. B. (2006). "She was family": Women of color and animal-human connections. *Affilia, 21*, 433–447. doi:10.1177/0886109906292314

Risley-Curtiss, C., Holley, L. C., & Wolf, S. (2006). The animal-human bond and ethnic diversity. *Social Work, 51*, 257–268.

Risley-Curtiss, C., Rogge, M. E., & Kawam, E. (2013). Factors affecting social workers' inclusion of animals in practice. *Social Work, 58*, 153–161. doi:10.1093/sw/swt009

Rockett, B., & Carr, S. (2014). Animals and attachment theory. *Society & Animals, 22*, 415–424.

Rogelberg, S. G., DiGiacomo, N., Reeve, C. L., Spitzmüller, C., Clark, O. L., Teeter, L., et al. (2007). What shelters can do about euthanasia-related stress: An examination of recommendations from those on the front line. *Journal of Applied Animal Welfare Science, 10*, 331–347. doi:10.1080/10888700701353865

Rosenkoetter, M. M. (1991). Health promotion: The influence of pets on life patterns in the home. *Holistic Nursing Practice, 5*(2), 42–51.

Rowan, A. N., & Beck, A. M. (1994). The health benefits of human-animal interactions. *Anthrozoös, 7*, 85–89.

Rujoiu, O., & Rujoiu, V. (2013). Human-animal bond: Loss and grief. A review of the literature. *Social Work Review/Revista De Asistenţă Socială, 12*(3), 163–171.

Russow, L. M. (2002). Ethical implications of the human-animal bond in the laboratory. *ILAR Journal, 43*, 33–37.

Ryan, T. (2011). *Animals and social work: A moral introduction*. Hampshire, United Kingdom: Palgrave Macmillan.

Ryan, T. (Ed.). (2014). *Animals in social work: Why and how they matter*. Hampshire, United Kingdom: Palgrave Macmillan.

Ryder, E. L. (1985). Pets and the elderly: A social work perspective. *Veterinary Clinics of North America: Small Animal Practice, 15*, 333–343.

Ryder, E., & Romasco, M. (1981). Establishing a social work service in a veterinary hospital. In B. Fogle (Ed.), *Interrelations between people and pets* (pp. 209–220). Springfield, IL: C. C. Thomas.

Sable, P. (1995). Pets, attachment, and well-being across the life cycle. *Social Work, 40,* 334–341.

Safe Humane Chicago. (n.d.). *Lifetime bonds.* Retrieved from http://www .safehumanechicago.org/programs/lifetime-bonds

Scott, C. (2008). *Pawprints of Katrina: Pets saved and lessons learned.* Hoboken, NJ: Wiley.

Searchers try to reunite boy, dog. (2005, September 6). *Fox News.* Retrieved from http://www.foxnews.com/story/2005/09/06/searchers-try-to-reunite-boy-dog.html

Serpell, J. A. (1991). Beneficial effects of pet ownership on some aspects of human health and behaviour. *Journal of the Royal Society of Medicine, 84,* 717–720.

Serpell, J. A. (2010). Animal companions and human well-being: An historical exploration of the value of human–animal relationships. In A. H. Fine (Ed.), *Handbook on animal-assisted therapy: Theoretical foundations and guidelines for practice* (3rd ed., pp. 17–32). London: Academic Press.

Serpell, J. A. (2011). Historical and cultural perspectives on human-pet interactions. In P. McCardle, S. McCune, J. Griffin, L. Esposito, & L. Freund (Eds.), *Animals in our lives: Human–animal interaction in family, community, and therapeutic settings* (pp. 11–22). Baltimore: Brookes.

Serpell, J. A., Coppinger, R., Fine, A. H., & Peralta, J. M. (2010). Welfare consideration in therapy and assistance animals. In A. H. Fine (Ed.), *Handbook on animal-assisted therapy: Theoretical foundations and guidelines for practice* (3rd ed., pp. 481–504). London: Academic Press.

Serpell, J. A., & McCune, S. (2012). *The Waltham pocket book of human-animal interactions.* Leicestershire, United Kingdom: Beyond Design Solutions.

Service Dog Central. (n.d.-a). *Types of working dogs.* Retrieved October 13, 2016, from http://servicedogcentral.org/content/node/280

Service Dog Central. (n.d.-b). *Welcome to Service Dog Central.* Retrieved October 13, 2016, from http://servicedogcentral.org/content/

Shanan, A., August, K., Cooney, K., Hendrix, L., Mader, B., & Pierce, J. (2014). *Animal hospice and palliative care guidelines.* Retrieved from https://www.iaahpc.org/images/IAAHPCGUIDELINESMarch14.pdf

Shapiro, K., & Henderson, A.J.Z. (2016). *The identification, assessment, and treatment of adults who abuse animals: The AniCare Approach.* New York: Springer.

Shapiro, K., Randour, M. L., Krinsk, S., & Wolf, J. L. (2014). *The assessment and treatment of children who abuse animals: The AniCare Child Approach.* New York: Springer.

Sheade, H., & Chandler, C. (2012, November). *Cultural diversity considerations in animal assisted counseling.* Paper presented at the Texas Counseling Association Conference, Galveston, TX.

Shir-Vertesh, D. (2012). "Flexible personhood": Loving animals as family members in Israel. *American Anthropologist, 114,* 420–432. doi:10.1111/j.1548-1433.2012.01443.x

Siegel, J. M. (1990). Stressful life events and use of physician services among the elderly: The moderating role of pet ownership. *Journal of Personality and Social Psychology, 58,* 1081–1086.

Singer, P. (1975). *Animal liberation.* New York: Random House.

Singer, R. S., Hart, L. A., & Zasloff, R. L. (1995). Dilemmas associated with rehousing homeless people who have companion animals. *Psychological Reports, 77,* 851–857.

Slatter, J., Lloyd, C., & King, R. (2012). Homelessness and companion animals: More than just a pet? *British Journal of Occupational Therapy, 75,* 377–383. doi:10.4276/030802212X13433105374350

Slovenko, R. (1983). Human/companion animal bond and the anthropomorphizing and naming of pets. *Medicine and Law, 2,* 277–283.

Smith, B. (2012). The 'pet effect': Health related aspects of companion animal ownership. *Australian Family Physician, 41,* 439–442.

Social diversity. (n.d.). Retrieved from https://www.reference.com/world-view/social-diversity-32474254a8c3dce2

Staats, S. W., Wallace, H., & Anderson, T. (2008). Reasons for companion animal guardianship (pet ownership) from two populations. *Society and Animals, 16,* 279–291.

Steketee, G., Gibson, A., Frost, R. O., Alabiso, J., Arluke, A., & Patronek, G. (2011). Characteristics and antecedents of people who hoard animals: An exploratory comparative interview study. *Review of General Psychology, 15,* 114–124.

Stroebe, M. S., Hansson, R. O., Schut, H. E., Stroebe, W. E., & Van den Blink, E. I. (2008). *Handbook of bereavement research and practice:*

Advances in theory and intervention. Washington, DC: American Psychological Association.

Tapia, F. (1971). Children who are cruel to animals. *Child Psychiatry and Human Development, 2*(2), 70–77.

Taylor, N., Fraser, H., Signal, T., & Prentice, K. (2016). Social work, animal-assisted therapies and ethical considerations: A programme example from Central Queensland, Australia. *British Journal of Social Work, 46,* 135–152. doi:10.1093/bjsw/bcu115

Tedeschi, P., Fitchett, J., & Molidor, C. E. (2005). The incorporation of animal-assisted interventions in social work education. *Journal of Family Social Work, 9*(4), 59–77.

Tiesman, H. M., Konda, S., Hartley, D., Menéndez, C. C., Ridenour, M., & Hendricks, S. (2015). Suicide in U.S. workplaces, 2003–2010: A comparison with non-workplace suicides. *American Journal of Preventive Medicine, 48,* 674–682. doi:10.1016/j.amepre.2014.12.011

Tipper, B. (2011). 'A dog who I know quite well': Everyday relationships between children and animals. *Children's Geographies, 9,* 145–165. doi:10.1080/14733285.2011.562378

Toledo Area Humane Society. (1884). *Annual report of the Toledo Area Humane Society.* Toledo, OH: Comly & Francisco Book and Job.

Toledo Area Humane Society. (1894). *Annual report of the Toledo Area Humane Society.* Toledo, OH: Hadley & Hadley.

Toledo Area Humane Society. (n.d.). *Behavior helpline.* Retrieved from https://www.toledohumane.org/behavior-helpline

Toray, T. (2004). The human-animal bond and loss: Providing support for grieving clients. *Journal of Mental Health Counseling, 26,* 244–259.

Trauma. (n.d.). In *Dictionary.com unabridged.* Retrieved from http://www.dictionary.com/browse/trauma

Turner, W. G. (2003). Bereavement counseling: Using a social work model for pet loss. *Journal of Family Social Work, 7*(1), 69–81. doi:10.1300/J039v07n01_05

Turner, W. G. (2005). The role of companion animals throughout the family life cycle. *Journal of Family Social Work, 9*(4), 11–21. doi:10.1300/J039v09n04_02

University of Denver Graduate School of Social Work. (n.d.). *Animal-assisted social work certificate.* Retrieved from http://www.du.edu/

socialwork/programs/oncampus/twoyear/certificates/aaswcerti
ficate.html

U.S. Department of Justice, Civil Rights Division. (2011). *ADA 2010
revised requirements: Service animals*. Retrieved from https://www
.ada.gov/service_animals_2010.htm

U.S. Department of Justice, Civil Rights Division. (2015). *Frequently
asked questions about service animals and the ADA*. Retrieved from
https://www.ada.gov/regs2010/service_animal_qa.html

Vagnoli, L., Caprilli, S., Vernucci, C., Zagni, S., Mugnai, F., & Messeri,
A. (2015). Can presence of a dog reduce pain and distress in children during venipuncture? *Pain Management Nursing, 16*, 89–95.
doi:10.1016/j.pmn.2014.04.004

Vaughn, M. G., Fu, Q., DeLisi, M., Beaver, K. M., Perron, B. E., Terrell,
K., & Howard, M. O. (2009). Correlates of cruelty to animals in the
United States: Results from the National Epidemiologic Survey on
Alcohol and Related Conditions. *Journal of Psychiatric Research, 43*,
1213–1218. doi:10.1016/j.jpsychires.2009.04.011

Villalobos, A. E. (2011). Quality-of-life assessment techniques for veterinarians. *Veterinary Clinics of North America: Small Animal Practice,
41*, 519–529.

Walker, P., Aimers, J., & Perry, C. (2015). Animals and social work: An emerging field of practice for Aotearoa New Zealand. *Aotearoa New Zealand
Social Work, 27*(1–2), 24–35. doi:10.11157/anzswj-vol27iss1-2id14

Walsh, F. (2009a). Human-animal bonds I: The relational significance of
companion animals. *Family Process, 48*, 462–480. doi:10.1111/j.1545-
5300.2009.01296.x

Walsh, F. (2009b). Human-animal bonds II: The role of pets in family systems and family therapy. *Family Process, 48*, 481–499. doi:10.1111/
j.1545-5300.2009.01297.x

Walton-Moss, B. J., Manganello, J., Frye, V., & Campbell, J. C. (2005). Risk
factors for intimate partner violence and associated injury among
urban women. *Journal of Community Health, 30*, 377–389.

Watkins, S. A. (1990). The Mary Ellen myth: Correcting child welfare
history. *Social Work, 35*, 500–503.

Weiss, R. (1974). The provisions of social relationships. In Z. Rubin (Ed.),
Doing unto others (pp. 17–26). Englewood Cliffs, NJ: Prentice-Hall.

Williams, B. (2014). Animal hoarding: Devastating, complex, and everyone's concern. *Mental Health Practice, 17*(6), 35–39.

Wilson, C. C., Netting, F. E., Turner, D. C., & Olsen, C. H. (2013). Companion animals in obituaries: An exploratory study. *Anthrozoös, 26,* 227–236. doi:10.2752/175303713X13636846944204

Wisch, R. F. (2015). *FAQs on emotional support animals.* Retrieved from https://www.animallaw.info/article/faqs-emotional-support-animals#s3

Wisdom, J. P., Saedi, G. A., & Green, C. A. (2009). Another breed of "service" animals: STARS study findings about pet ownership and recovery from serious mental illness. *American Journal of Orthopsychiatry, 79,* 430–436. doi:10.1037/a0016812

Wogan, J. B. (2013, July 26). Connecticut may be 1st state to codify animal-assisted therapy for trauma victims [Blog post]. Retrieved from http://www.governing.com/blogs/view/gov-animal-assisted-therapy-law-connecticut.html

Wolf, D. B. (2000). Social work and speciesism [Commentary]. *Social Work, 45,* 88–93.

Wood, L., Giles-Corti, B., & Bulsara, M. K. (2005). The pet connection: Pets as a conduit for social capital? *Social Science & Medicine, 61,* 1159–1173. doi:10.1016/j.socscimed.2005.01.017

Wood, L. J., Giles-Corti, B., Bulsara, M. K., & Bosch, D. A. (2007). More than a furry companion: The ripple effect of companion animals on neighborhood interactions and sense of community. *Society & Animals, 15,* 43–56. doi:10.1163/156853007X169333

Wood, L., Martin, K., Christian, H., Nathan, A., Lauritsen, C., Houghton, S., et al. (2015). The pet factor: Companion animals as a conduit for getting to know people, friendship formation and social support. *PloS ONE, 10*(4), Article e0122085. doi:10.1371/journal.pone.0122085

Yorke, J., Adams, C., & Coady, N. (2008). Therapeutic value of equine-human bonding in recovery from trauma. *Anthrozoös, 21,* 17–30. doi:10.2752/089279308X274038

Zastrow, C. H., & Kirst-Ashman, K. K. (2007). *Understanding human behavior and the social environment.* Belmont, CA: Brooks/Cole.

Zilcha-Mano, S., Mikulincer, M., & Shaver, P. R. (2011). An attachment perspective on human–pet relationships: Conceptualization and assessment of pet attachment orientations. *Journal of Research in Personality, 45,* 345–357.

Zilney, L. A., & Zilney, M. (2005). Reunification of child and animal welfare agencies: Cross-reporting of abuse in Wellington County, Ontario. *Child Welfare, 84,* 47–66.

Zimolag, U., & Krupa, T. (2010). The occupation of pet ownership as an enabler of community integration in serious mental illness: A single exploratory case study. *Occupational Therapy in Mental Health, 26,* 176–196.

Zottarelli, L. K. (2010). Broken bond: An exploration of human factors associated with companion animal loss during Hurricane Katrina. *Sociological Forum, 25,* 110–122. doi:10.1111/j.1573-7861.2009.01159.x

INDEX